101 Ways to
Recession-Proof
Your Career

101 Ways to Recession-Proof Your Career

Wendy S. Enelow, CPRW, JCTC, CCM

McGraw-Hill

New York   Chicago   San Francisco   Lisbon   London
Madrid   Mexico City   Milan   New Delhi
San Juan   Seoul   Singapore
Sydney   Toronto

McGraw-Hill

A Division of The **McGraw·Hill** Companies

1 2 3 4 5 6 7 8 9 0   DOC/DOC   0 9 8 7 6 5 4 3 2

ISBN 0-07-139847-3

This book was set in Minion by Binghamton Valley Composition.

Printed and bound by R. R. Donnelley & Sons Company.

This publication is designed to provide accurate and authoritative information in regard to the subject matter covered. It is sold with the understanding that the publisher is not engaged in rendering legal, accounting, or other professional service. If legal advice or other expert assistance is required, the services of a competent professional person should be sought.

— From a declaration of principles jointly adopted by a committee of the American Bar Association and a committee of publishers.

 This book is printed on recycled, acid-free paper containing a minimum of 50% recycled, de-inked fiber.

McGraw-Hill books are available at special quantity discounts to use as premiums and sales promotions, or for use in corporate training programs. For more information, please write to the Director of Special Sales, Professional Publishing, McGraw-Hill, Two Penn Plaza, New York, NY 10121-2298. Or contact your local bookstore.

This book is dedicated to the thousands and thousands of career professionals worldwide who have devoted their careers to helping others succeed in theirs. And, to the 48 career experts who contributed to this publication, I thank you for sharing your expertise with me and with job seekers around the globe. This book would not have been possible, or nearly as valuable, without your knowledge, expertise, and individual contributions.

Contents

INTRODUCTION

It's Not a Recession . . .
It's an Opportunity!

You will always be faced with opportunities brilliantly disguised as problems and challenges.

(Susan Guarneri—2001)

Between 1995 and 2000, we watched with delight as the economy soared and employment was strong. We felt great! Then, starting in late 2000 and early 2001, our economy began to slow and there was much talk about a pending recession. We held our breath and hoped that those predicting the recession were wrong and that things would bounce right back. However, as we got further into 2001, things were not looking good.

We watched with amazement, and a bit of horror, as some of the nation's most steadfast and prominent companies (e.g., Xerox Corp., DaimlerChrysler, Lucent Technologies) along with many of the newer dot-com and technology firms (e.g., Enron, Gateway, Amazon.com, Ericsson), cut their workforces by thousands.

Other companies, battling to keep their workforces in place, introduced a diversity of cost-cutting measures:

- One of the world's leaders in the investment community introduced a new policy requiring employees to take three Fridays off, without pay, every two months.
- A global technology company is requiring all employees to travel coach on domestic flights and stay in budget hotels.
- One of the nation's oldest insurance companies starting charging their employees for what used to be free coffee and tea.
- A major office machines manufacturer requested that their employees make photocopies only when absolutely necessary.

Then it was September 11 and everything changed forever. In those first few weeks, most of us forgot about the recession, our own personal employment situations, and so much more. We hoped and we prayed for those in the World Trade Center, the Pentagon, and the open field in Shanksville, Pennsylvania. All of a sudden, our individual employment situations weren't quite as important. In fact, on a televised interview, a displaced "blue-collar" worker from an aerospace manufacturer spoke with tears in his eyes as he told the reporter that he was sorry to have lost his job, but that it was a very small price to pay. It was a dramatic moment; two weeks earlier that same individual would, most likely, have been angry and bitter. Not any more. We have all reprioritized and put our work lives in a much better and healthier context. Work is vital, yet it is by no means all that there is to life.

As we struggled to reclaim our lives and find the "new normal," the recession and dramatic toll it was going to take on our employment market hit us head on. It was not a question of if there would be a recession or when it would happen. It was now. If we had been teetering on the brink of recession, September 11 pushed us way over the edge and we are now in a full-blown economic crisis.

In the last quarter of 2001, we watched as hundreds of thousands of people were displaced from their jobs—from the warehouse manager at Boeing to the pilot at American Airlines; from the secretary at the software design company to the financial consultant at a major investment firm. The recession has hit virtually every sector of our economy with a particularly devastating impact on the technology, airline, and finance/banking industries. We're reeling from the blow, the double-digit losses in our financial markets, and the continued downturn of what we had previously thought of as "recession-proof" industries and professions. No one has been left unscathed and, unfortunately, the reality is that the recession will continue at least for the immediate future.

The result of all this is that employees are running scared. Most would rather take a small pay cut or reduction in their benefits than leave their current jobs and look elsewhere. But, you don't need to run scared! Although we are constantly hearing about layoffs, cutbacks, recession, and more, there are thousands and thousands of opportunities that exist. The questions you must ask yourself are how you can manage your work life in spite of the recession, take advantage of the opportunities that do exist (there really are some!), and continue to move your career forward.

The answers to those questions and many more are what you will find in this book—the 101 *best* strategies to recession-proof your career. As you read through, you'll learn how to:

- Take control of your career and your career destiny.
- Prepare yourself for a successful job search and a life of career satisfaction.
- Write winning resumes, cover letters, follow-up letters, career portfolios, and more.
- Plan and manage a successful job search campaign.
- Improve your networking skills and results.
- Strengthen your interviewing performance.
- Negotiate your best salary and compensation plan.
- Proactively manage your career throughout your entire work life-cycle.

"Every day we must continue to earn the right to keep our positions."
(Meg Montford—2001)

The development of this book has been a joint effort among 49 career professionals—career coaches, career counselors, resume writers, outplacement consultants, recruiters, human resources professionals, and others. They joined together to create a practical guide that will give you the knowledge to manage your career effectively as the employment landscape continues to change as we move through and out of this recession. Take their advice to heart and you'll find that you are not a victim of the recession, but rather a true professional who knows how to manage your career in spite of the recession.

Many of the contributors to this book have earned distinguished professional credentials, certifications, and licenses. Here are some of the ones you'll see most frequently:

CCM	Credentialed Career Master
CEIP	Certified Employment Interview Professional
CIPC	Certified International Personnel Consultant
CMP	Career Management Professional
CPRW	Certified Professional Resume Writer
CRW	Certified Resume Writer
JCTC (or IJCTC)	Job and Career Transition Coach (International)
LPC	Licensed Professional Counselor
NCC	National Certified Counselor
NCCC	National Certified Career Counselor
NCRW	Nationally Certified Resume Writer
PCC	Professional Career Counselor
SPHR	Senior Professional in Human Resources

Top 10 Strategies to Recession-Proof Your Career

As you read all 101 of the recession-proofing strategies in this book, remember these top 10 strategies, for they are the foundation upon which all the other strategies are based. If you remember nothing else, remember these, for they are what will lead you to your own *career success.*

1. Take Control of Your Career Destiny
2. Find and Communicate Your Career Value
3. Use a Diversified Job Search Strategy
4. Communicate "Who" You Are
5. Write Powerful Career Marketing Communications
6. Follow-Up, Follow-Up, and Follow-Up
7. Networking Is Your #1 Search Strategy
8. Continue Learning, Growing, and Moving Forward
9. Know Your Financial Worth and Ask for It
10. Always Remember Who You Really Work for—*Yourself*

101 Ways to Recession-Proof Your Career

CHAPTER 1

Take Control of Your Career and Your Life

TIP #1—Take Control Now!

Taking control of your career and your career destiny requires just one thing—*action*.

First, you must release the old, preconceived image of what a career is supposed to be. What used to be, no longer is and never will be again. The chances of joining a company that you'll still be working for in 10, 15, or 20 years are virtually nil. Industries, companies, technologies, economic markets . . . everything is changing at a phenomenal rate. So are careers.

Today's career has a life cycle of its own. It changes and moves, often not staying too long in any one place. It is fluid and dynamic, responding to market changes and taking advantage of new employment opportunities. Once you understand and accept this concept, *your career will change*. Then it's up to you to take control and steer your career path in the direction that you want.

This does not mean that you must be engaged in an active job search campaign all of the time. What it does mean is that you must be prepared and have everything in place should you suddenly find yourself looking for a new job or should a great new job find you.

Follow these seven Key Action Steps to keep yourself prepared:

Step 1—Always have a current resume. You never know when a great opportunity may present itself and, if it does, you want to be instantly prepared and ready to respond.

Step 2—Update your resume with new skills, achievements, project highlights, and more, as they happen. This way, not only do you always have a current resume, you also have a living document with which to map your career.

Step 3—Stay in touch with your network. Send an email and make a quick phone call to your most important network contacts on an occasional basis, just to stay in touch. That way, when you find yourself engaged in an active job search, you're not just contacting these people when you need them.

Step 4—Stay in touch with recruiters you know and be sure that they always have a copy of your current resume. You never know when they might have a search assignment for a position that is ideal for you.

Step 5—Pay close attention to what's going on inside your company. Often there are subtle signs of impending change, both positive and negative. Be alert, but not paranoid.

Step 6—Watch economic trends in your industry to keep informed about long-term employment opportunities and stability.

Step 7—Post your resume on a select number of websites where you think you'll get the best response. This keeps your name visible within your industry or profession and may open the door to unknown opportunities. Note that many of these sites offer confidential postings so they can protect your identity and your current job. See Web Research and Information Tools at the end of Chapter 4 for a list of recommended websites.

Important Note: If you know that you are going to leave your current position, or if you're concerned about possible layoffs, downsizings, or reorganizations, you need to start a full-scale job search campaign now! This means doing all of these seven steps in addition to much more as outlined in Chapters 3 through 7. Don't wait until you've already left your position or the company has abandoned you. If you do, you'll experience too much downtime and too many missed opportunities.

—Author's tip

TIP #2—Don't Panic!

When the employment market takes a tumble, many people respond impulsively and tend to panic. Who can blame them? We all need our jobs and no one likes uncertainty. The problem, though, is that panic tends to prevent you from taking the measured steps necessary to solve the problem effectively, which only creates more panic. This insidious process feeds upon itself and can have seriously counterproductive, and even devastating, results.

In the employment world, the panic I'm speaking of can manifest itself in a variety of ways:

- Those who find themselves out of a job as the result of a recession frantically start a knee-jerk, job-hunting process with little focus or direction. They quickly update their resume, apply for every job they see advertised whether it's a good fit or not, call every recruiter in the phone book, and otherwise make rash and haphazard decisions.

- Those who are lucky enough to remain employed when the recession hits tend to hang on to their current job for dear life, even if they desperately hate what they're doing.

- Others are simply frozen and lose sight of what they were doing, where they were going, and, ultimately, don't or can't do anything at all.

Smart career management calls for a calculated and organized approach, and that still holds true even when you feel your back is against the wall. Here are a few suggestions to handle panic when you feel it approaching:

- *Vent and let it out!* If you feel your emotions rising and your head is filled with worries about everything that could possibly go wrong, your best bet is to let those feelings out before they cloud your judgment. Find someone positive and caring to talk to and release those feelings. This will clear room for more productive thinking and a more positive attitude.
- *Develop a plan.* If you remain frantic and unorganized, your results will quickly frustrate you. Consider what you need to accomplish and put together a plan of action with specific goals and action steps.
- *Get the help you need.* Follow the expert advice in this book and then, if you think it will help, contact a professional who can help you with your resume, job search strategy, and interviewing skills. Or you may consider contacting a friend or colleague who has successfully navigated an organized and successful job search in the past. There are great people out there who are willing to help you, so take advantage of the opportunities.
- *Don't lose sight of your goals.* Employment slowdowns are only temporary and do not mean that you can't get the job of your dreams. Channel any "panic" energy toward your goals and keep your eyes open for opportunities—you just might be thrilled with the results!

   —Ross Macpherson, MA, CPRW, CEIP, JCTC, Career Quest

TIP #3—STAY POSITIVE IN YOUR JOB SEARCH

Job search and career uncertainty can create mixed emotions of both excitement in a new future and fear of the unknown. By following a few simple principles, you'll find that the process will be much easier.

- *Do something nice for yourself.* Once a week, for at least two hours, take yourself on a date alone. Your date could involve taking a hike along a trail, going to a movie, browsing in a bookstore, going to a daytime ball game, or anything you enjoy but don't usually take the time to do. You may worry that you don't have the money to spend on a date. Look around and be creative. There are many free things to do if you are open and seek them out.

- *Don't isolate yourself.* Take a class, join a job support group, meet with a friend on a regular basis, or volunteer to work at your local food bank. It is easy to isolate yourself during a job search. Don't! You'll find your spirits are much higher if you keep yourself socially active.

- *Talk to people that you normally wouldn't.* Ask different people about their work, strike up a conversation at the grocery store, and take time to develop or reconnect with a network contact. Networking is not only a great job search tool, but also a way to genuinely listen to what others do in their worlds of work. You may be surprised where your next job lead comes from.

- *Expose yourself to what you don't know.* Your job search will follow what you know. Now is a time to expand your horizons and learn about what others do beyond your scope of reference. By exposing yourself to new areas, you will expose yourself to more opportunities.

- *Keep a journal.* Keeping a journal, as painful as this sounds, is a superb way to privately express yourself. It is a place to let go of your frustrations and a safe place to first expose a wild idea. Research has shown that job seekers who keep a journal land a new position sooner. Keeping a journal gives you a forum of expression to think about what you really want in your future and what has frustrated you in the past. Committing your thoughts to paper can have an amazing impact on your ability to move forward toward the life you want to create.

Above all, believe in yourself as a competent, capable person, knowing that the right position is also looking for you.

—Susan Luff Chritton, M.Ed., NCCC, CRPCC, Pathways/Right Management Consultants

TIP #4—BE FLEXIBLE

When faced with a declining economic climate and a job market flooded with candidates, flexibility becomes extremely critical. Before its downturn in November 2000, the market was ruled by job seekers. If their skills warranted, they could wield quite a bit of negotiating power over an employer desperate for qualified talent. In a recessionary environment, however, job seekers typically don't have as many choices and must be more flexible with their expectations.

The "one size fits all" approach of generic resume and cover letter writing won't work in a tight labor market. You must be willing to create a more customized approach with your resume and cover letter presentation, honing in on each individual employer's needs and fully illustrating your credentials, core competencies, and capacity to provide solutions and make an immediate impact. Job seekers in direct revenue-generating roles are usually a hotter commodity than those in more operationally geared or support-related positions. If skills are lacking in some areas, you should recognize that additional training may be required in order to get up to speed. Employers don't have the luxury of hiring someone who requires a significant learning curve. Rather, they need personnel who can hit the ground running and begin to produce results immediately.

You should also be open to the idea of changing careers if the market has had a particularly dramatic impact on your industry. Following the tragedy of September 11, companies in the travel, hospitality, and airline industries saw their revenues drop by as much as 50 percent. With no expectation that these industries would rebound quickly, many job seekers looked beyond their titles to uncover the skills that could easily be transferred to other types of positions in other industries.

In the hunt itself, you will have better luck when you rely on more traditional means to uncover opportunities. The Internet has revealed itself as a wonderful tool, but it is only one among many in the arsenal. Networking remains the most effective method used to secure a new position, and you must recognize the need to step up your networking efforts as much as possible.

Finally, you may also have to be flexible with regard to initial salary offering, core job responsibilities, and the possibility of accepting a job you may consider to be beneath your capabilities, just to establish yourself within a new organization. If looked upon as a short-term solution, this could be exactly the break you need to solidify your future advancement as soon as the economic climate improves.

—*E. René Hart, CPRW, Executive Career Solutions*

TIP #5—SHARPEN YOUR TECHNICAL SKILLS

Remember the IBM Selectric II typewriter—the one with autocorrection. It was revolutionary in its day. Then along came the first word processors and we marveled at the efficiency of the Mag Card and Vydec. We thought we'd arrived! Just after we mastered them, the PC arrived and, since then, we've all been working to keep pace with changing technologies, software programs, networks, the Internet, email, and more.

If you happen to be a "techie" person, you've most likely found all of these changes fun and exciting. We all know these kinds of people—they get excited when new electronic gadgets hit the market, spend hours experimenting with new computer programs, and actually read the directions that come with new devices!

However, the rest of us—the "non-techie" crowd—often struggle to keep pace. Just as we mastered Word Star, along came WordPerfect. Once that was under our belts, virtually the entire world transitioned to Microsoft Word. And, we won't even talk about the issues surrounding the Mac versus the PC. It's exhausting. Just give us something that works, show us how to use it, and then let it be. But, alas, in the ever-changing world of technology, this is not meant to be!

To win in job search, each and every job seeker today must be PC proficient. Why?

1. Virtually every job requires that you use a PC. It's that simple. Whether you're a nurse posting medical results to a patient's online file, a construction superintendent monitoring job costs, or a sales rep keeping track of all of your customer accounts on your laptop and Palm Pilot, technology is a part of each and every job. There is no getting around it.

2. So much of the job process and so many job search tools are now technology based. You'll want to post your resume on the Internet, email your resume as a Word attachment to some companies and as a text file to others, and maybe even decide to develop your own website as part of your career marketing campaign.

If you're not PC and Internet savvy, consider taking a course or two at your local PC training center or community college. The cost shouldn't be prohibitive, and the time you invest will pay for itself over and over in increasing your attractiveness to prospective employers and raising your income.

—Author's tip

TIP #6—COMMUNICATE YOUR CAREER VALUE

News of layoffs across many sectors of the U.S. economy has employed workers wondering if they should stay put and weather the storm. Unemployed job seekers, forced to look during tough times, often struggle. One group of job seekers, however, is successful regardless of the economic climate. These individuals understand company needs and can successfully communicate their value to potential employers.

A friend, Joe, recently was downsized from his longtime position as president of North American operations for an international manufacturer. I heard about it from another friend a couple of days after it happened and called Joe to offer support. I was concerned he might have some difficulty getting another job because he was in a small market, was close to retirement age, and had never completed his degree. However, he was upbeat and mentioned that he had been in contact with several colleagues to let them know about his situation and had already received two offers. He told me that he was flying out of town the next day to check out another exciting opportunity that he had read about in a trade magazine. I caught up with him a few days later when he returned from the interview. He was offered the job and had accepted. Joe's unemployment lasted less than one week.

Another friend, Sue, was downsized from her job as PR director for a wireless communication firm. Soon after being laid off, she consulted with me and updated her resume. She told me that she had a number of companies in mind and was going to get her resume right out to them. About a month later, I checked in with her to see how her search was progressing. "Well, I sent my resume to about seven companies advertising on the Internet, but I haven't heard back from any of them. Then, the one guy I spoke with on the phone didn't care at all about what I wanted to tell him. It was a disaster."

So, what is the difference between Joe and Sue? Is it luck? Perhaps, but probably not. Judging each based on resume statistics alone, Sue should have had the upper hand. Her experience is in a rapidly expanding industry; she's young, energetic, and well-educated; and she has led many successful, revenue-producing projects. Sue, like many job seekers, believes that her resume speaks for her and that "it should be obvious" what she can do for an employer. Joe, on the other hand, does not have as impressive of a resume, but has mastered the art of communicating his value to every person with whom he comes in contact.

Job seekers who understand how to demonstrate their value will find many job opportunities, regardless of the economy. And, as employers begin to focus more heavily on bottom-line results, the prospective employee who can document and communicate results and success will have a remarkable advantage over other candidates.

This concept of demonstrating value can be applied to every step of the job search process and should be continued once the offer has been made and accepted. When researching potential firms, look for companies that are committed to delivering a valuable product or service. When developing a resume and cover letter, highlight all areas where you added value by expanding sales, increasing productivity, generating positive goodwill, and/or reducing expenses. In the interview and subsequent salary negotiations, speak about your ability to deliver bottom-line contributions, embrace change, and make things happen.

Most importantly, remember that value—extrinsic or intrinsic—is just as much an attitude as it is a measurable statistic!

—Michele Haffner, CPRW, JCTC, Advanced Resume Services

TIP #7—Develop the Right Attitude

J. F. Kennedy said ". . . ask not what your country can do for you; ask what you can do for your country." Now, replace the word *country* with *company* and you have the key to success in developing a powerful resume, acing the interview, climbing the corporate ladder of success, and, ultimately, recession-proofing your career.

It's all in your attitude—whether it's the tone of your resume and cover letter, your demeanor during an interview, or your comments about the company you currently work for. Many company executives have stated that when presented with two similarly qualified candidates, they will usually select the candidate with a dynamic attitude and strong interpersonal skills. It is those qualifications which are critical in building a strong team to achieve the company's goals.

What is attitude? It's your beliefs and the way you think. Your thoughts and beliefs are communicated in the way you walk, your choice of words, the tone of your voice and written communications, the way you present yourself, your level of enthusiasm, your facial expressions, and your body language. So, attitude begins with the thoughts in your mind and is then externalized.

Consider two salespeople, Janice and Aaron, selling the same product for two different companies. Aaron believes that since the economy is in a recession, none of his clients will want to buy any products because businesses are laying off and money is tight. Aaron continues his usual selling routine and sure enough, customers aren't buying. Eventually, Aaron gives up on sales and takes a job for less money just so he can pay the bills.

Janice has a totally different attitude. She knows that she is going to have to work harder to identify and sell clients, so she develops several unique prospecting and sales closing strategies. She believes that even during a recession, companies will purchase her product because she has positioned it as a product that will help their company survive. She is amazed at how impassive her competition is and how few of them are in the field. Janice far exceeds her company's quotas. Her positive attitude is the driving force.

Changing your attitude begins by changing your thoughts and beliefs. Begin to think of yourself as an independent consultant—one who provides services to accomplish a particular corporate initiative or project. When the initiative or project is complete, the contract between the consultant and the company is fulfilled, and the consultant moves on to another project (a.k.a. job) requiring her expertise.

To identify the services you will provide, start by identifying your distinguishing talents and skills. What have you consistently focused on and accomplished throughout your career? Which talents and skills provided you with a feeling of fulfillment? What have been your most triumphant moments? Write down the thoughts that immediately come to mind. Then, tuck that list in your pocket and review it every day. Continue to add to your list whenever more thoughts come to mind.

Once you have a substantial list, reflect on each entry and identify the skills, abilities, and knowledge areas involved in each of your accomplishments and successes. These are your unique talents. Yes, others may have many of the same talents. However, each person has a unique combination of hundreds of skills, abilities, and talents. These are the unique contributions you will be selling to prospective employers.

When you have the right attitude and approach a company about offering your services (a.k.a. an interview), you'll be well-equipped to discuss the value you bring to the table and the contributions you can make to the company's success. Your new attitude will be sending a clear and self-confident message that you are a dynamic contributor.

—*Beverly Harvey, CPRW, JCTC, CCM, Beverly Harvey Resume & Career Services*

TIP #8—BEING DOWNSIZED CAN BE A GIFT!

Being downsized shakes up your usual routine and gives you the opportunity to look at your career and your life.

As a career counselor and corporate trainer, I see so many people do what they think they're supposed to do, what others told them they should do, what they think will make them money, what they fell into, or what was easy. As a result, I see too many people trapped in a lifetime of career unhappiness—the *right* people in the *wrong* jobs!

You know you're the right person in the right job when you love all the hard work and responsibility that goes with it. Each of us has a unique blending of skills, interests, personality, and values that can guide us to finding our vocation or career. The best match is a career that allows you to be yourself. When Leonardo da Vinci was asked to name his greatest accomplishment, he answered, "Leonardo da Vinci."

Those who find happiness in their careers share four common characteristics:

1. *Inner-direction.* They know themselves well. They are not so quick to believe well-meaning friends or family who say, "You can't do that." Ask yourself:
   - What are my special talents? What is my area of excellence?
   - What is it that I love? What would I do without financial reward?
   - What comes easy to me, but is difficult for someone else?

Then, use that information as the key to your competitive advantage over other job candidates.

2. *Passionate desire for something they wanted to attain or accomplish in their life.* They "saw a vision" of what they wanted to do. Ask yourself:
   - What do I want out of life?
   - How will I know when I get it?

That passionate desire or dream is critical; it's the "gas that keeps the car going." Being what we want to be and doing what we want to do with our lives doesn't just happen. Dreams are made real one step at a time over the long haul. From the first to the last, you will need focus, persistence, and the ability to keep in sight the vision of what you are slowly creating. Get excited about your dream!

3. *Commitment to personal excellence.* These people stretched beyond their comfort zone and grew. They acquired new skills and knowledge, keeping up with change. Unless you attempt to do something beyond what you have already mastered, you will never grow. Life is about challenge and growth. You will always be faced with opportunities brilliantly disguised as problems and challenges.

4. *Take action and refuse to fail.* I'm not saying they didn't fail, but they looked upon their failures as learning experiences and persisted in pursuing their goals. A lot of people I see who are successful and happy in their careers aren't people who had business contacts or were Rhodes scholars or computer whiz kids. They believed they could "do it"—they reached a little higher—and they succeeded in reaching their goals (sometimes against incredible odds). Believe in the power of believing in yourself.

Envision your dream and then act on it! That is the last and most critical element. Will Rogers once said, "Even if you're on the right track, you'll get run over if you just sit there."

Being downsized does *not* have to be a disaster. In fact, it can be the beginning of a whole *new* (and better) life!

—*Susan Guarneri, NCCC, NCC, LPC, JCTC, CPRW, CEIP,*
CCM, Guarneri Associates/Resumagic

TIP #9—CLIMB AHEAD

Do you ever wonder why some people are climbers and others are not? Why some people seem to have a natural ability to succeed no matter what the economic climate? What is different about these people? What is their magic formula?

It is simple: Climbers know the difference between their identity ("who they are") and their role ("what they are"). And they don't allow their identity and role to overlap.

Climbers are aware that their identity never changes. What does change are the roles they play. At work they are a manager, at home a spouse, and at soccer games a parent. If they have an off day in one role, they don't allow that to manipulate who they are as an individual.

Here is a crash course on how a climber responds to challenges. Mastering the following life lessons will help bridge the gap so that you can successfully cross over.

- *Don't internalize positive and negative events.* Don't define yourself by events that occur in your life. Successes or failures should not dictate who you are as a person.

- *Learn to accept failure.* The fear of rejection will hold you back from conducting a successful job search campaign. Disappointments are a part of our growth process. In the employment game, you get only two answers: "Yes, there seems to be a fit" or "No, there doesn't seem to be a fit." When you go on interviews, expect both responses.

- *Be responsive to change.* If you don't embrace change, fear, anger, and frustration, each will impede your job search. Anger might cause you to make quick and rash decisions. Frustration might lead you to give up on your job search just short of a breakthrough. And fear can paralyze you before your job search campaign ever begins.

- *Work through adversity.* Become your own cheerleader. When it comes down to it, you must be able to pick yourself up.

- *Accept responsibility.* Take ownership of the part you may have played in losing your job, forgive yourself, and move on.

- *Be patient.* Finding the right fit takes time. Becoming impatient leaves room for error in judgment. Wait for an opportunity that fits your career objective.

- *Don't look back; you are not going that way.* Don't get stuck in the "Why me?" stage. Focus on the steps you need to move forward. Distinguish between your immediate and long-term goals, and manage a focused employment campaign.

- *Avoid making unfair comparisons.* Clearly establish your goals and rate your success according to your own personal attitude, goals, and accomplishments.

- *Be consistent.* Create an aggressive action plan and make a commitment to follow through. In doing so, you position yourself as the key player in your future success.

It can be easy to fall into a victimized state after an economic downswing. Realize that nothing can affect your identity unless you relinquish control of who you are. Career success is a *choice*. Choose to be resilient, successful, and most importantly, a climber.

—*Linda Matias, JCTC, CEIP, CareerStrides*

TIP #10—LIVING AND WORKING ON THE EDGE OF CHANGE

Keith, a sales professional at a manufacturing company, was surprised when his position was eliminated. He had noticed that his division was slowing down and that all business development efforts were suspended six months earlier. However, he concluded that the situation was beyond his control, and Keith decided that the best he could do was to "lie low and see what comes next." Keith had never updated his skills or even identified other industries where his skills could be applied. When he was ultimately laid off, Keith didn't know where to begin and had a tough time finding new employment.

In contrast, his colleague, Susan, continually remained one step ahead of the curve. Not only did she heed the early warning signs in her company and study global industry trends, but she actively diversified her personal career portfolio by developing new skills. Through ongoing situational assessment and research, she became knowledgeable of other industries to which she could transfer her qualifications.

Consequently, Susan was well aware of both internal (within the company) and external (other companies and industries) career options along with her unique collection of skills, accomplishments, and experience so that she could launch her search in advance of the reduction in force.

Whose M.O. do you follow—Keith's or Susan's?

Today's ever-changing business climate requires vigilance in managing your work life. In fact, the basis of successful career management is the process of dealing with continual change. Nothing can equip you better to manage change than adopting the strategy of situational assessment—an understanding and awareness of the total environment. It's an integral part of every pilot's training. By incorporating situational assessment in your career management, you ensure your own career resilience.

Think of yourself as an entrepreneur and your career as the great new product you have for sale. Similar to any entrepreneur, you wear a number of hats that range from research and development to marketing and senior management.

For example, as R&D manager, you diversify your product offerings, develop new or improved versions of your products, and identify applications for your product's use. As product manager, you need to understand how your product measures up to the competition, what its features and benefits include, and how to price it effectively. As marketing director, you must be constantly alert to industry trends— in both your industry as well as others. You also need to understand customer needs and market changes over time. As sales manager, you create visibility for your product, introduce it to the marketplace, identify potential buyers, and close the deal with customers. Finally, as CEO of your business, you're accountable for overall product quality and effectiveness.

It's all up to you to develop the business plan and strategy, articulate your guiding mission and values, and define your product identity. Through this combination of roles, you build a career that will satisfy and position you in the marketplace.

At the heart of this endeavor is situational awareness and knowledge of internal trends—within your company, department, division, or business unit—and external trends—your industry, related industries, and others. Become and, most importantly, remain informed about emerging trends both within and outside of your company through research, courses, seminars, professional/industry associations, business publications, and other sources.

By taking a proactive approach to keep abreast of the "big picture" and assuming control over shaping your working life, you can plan proactively for a new job, occupational direction, or industry change, and avert being caught unexpectedly in the tides of change without a lifeline.

—*Louise Garver, MA, CMP, JCTC, CPRW, Career Directions*

TIP #11—GIVE THANKS

When you're at your lowest point, frustrated with your job search and feeling blue, remember to give thanks for all that you have. Your list might start with the nontangible things in your life—your family, friends, pets, church community, and more. Then, add in the tangible things—the house you worked for years to buy, the car that you love, your new kayak, and the wonderful Christmas card your 6-year-old child made for you. Remind yourself of the treasures that you already possess and then give thanks. What's more, remember to thank yourself, for much of what you have to be grateful for is a direct result of your hard work and effort.

This form of gratitude will energize you, give you a more positive outlook, and help you develop a clearer perspective, even during difficult times in your career. You'll be more confident, more creative, and able to work at your peak level of performance. You won't be as easily frustrated in your search campaign, and you'll regain control of your career. You'll be on top.

As you exude gratitude, you become a magnet that attracts positive outcomes and great new career opportunities. Just watch what happens!

—Author's tip

TIP #12—ALWAYS REMEMBER THAT LIFE IS MORE THAN WORK!

As you read through this book, as you plan and manage your job search, as you network, respond to advertisements, go on job interviews, and accept a new opportunity, always remember that life is more than just work.

When you're in the midst of a job search, you may find yourself overwhelmed with the process. In decades past it was easier. You simply mailed a few resumes in response to newspaper ads, made a few phone calls, and you were set. Today, you have to decide whether you need a career coach or not, whether to hire a professional resume writer and how to find one, how many websites you want to post your resume to, how to find recruiters in your industry, whether or not you need interview training, and so much more. The job search and career management processes have become vastly more complex and sophisticated. In turn, your options can be virtually unlimited and you often find yourself lost in the process of job search. The sections that follow in this book will give you clarity and lead you through each of these stages, showing you how to use each step to your advantage.

Because job search and career management can be time consuming and mentally exhausting, it is critical that you constantly remind yourself that your life is more than your job. Do not allow your career to overtake your entire life. Yes, it has a significant place in your life, but it is certainly not all that there is. Be sure to take a few steps back, breathe deeply, and try to put it all in perspective. A healthy mindset leads to a successful job search.

If you are depressed, no matter what you do to hide it, it will come through—in your words, your body language, and your behavior. No one wants to hire someone unless they're motivated, enthusiastic, and on top of their game. Don't allow yourself to fall into a negative mindset. Find support with your family, friends, coworkers, and others within your community. Then, work to overcome those feelings and get yourself back on track. That is where a career coach or career counselor can be of tremendous value to you. Not only do these professionals help you define your career path, they can help you address and resolve issues impeding your search.

Remember, maintaining the right perspective on how your career fits into your life is vital. Give your career the weight that it deserves and no more.

—*Author's tip*

CHAPTER 2

Planning and Preparing Yourself for Career Success

TIP #13—ASSEMBLE YOUR "SUCCESS TEAM"

It is extremely difficult to achieve your goals in isolation. Knowing this, successful people constantly surround themselves with other successful and positive people to support the realization of their goals. Your job search or career management goals are no different. You can either go it alone or benefit from the combined expertise and support of a team working with you to help you realize your goals.

In *Think & Grow Rich,* possibly the most influential book ever written on personal success, Napoleon Hill refers to assembling your "Master Mind"—a group of individuals coordinating both knowledge and effort "in a spirit of harmony" toward a common objective. In your case, that common objective is your career success.

Does this mean trying to gather a group of influential people together every week at the same time to discuss your future? Not necessarily. Chances are you will be assembling more of a virtual team of individuals that you can use as a resource. Each one may have a unique specialty or be able to help you in a specific way, and maybe you can meet them for lunch occasionally or arrange a phone call every two weeks. You have to develop a system that works for you and the respective members of your team. The point is to leverage the combined energy, motivation, and expertise of a group of individuals committed to helping you achieve success.

Specifically, how can your Success Team help you reach your career goals? Here's just a partial list of what they can do for you. They can:

- Help you develop a clear strategy and workable action plan
- Keep you positive in the face of challenges, obstacles, or adversity
- Help you stay on course and move in the right direction
- Provide you with sound advice and honest feedback
- Help you identify areas for improvement and/or professional development
- Help you set realistic goals and keep you accountable for them
- Provide you with a network of additional contacts that could help in your career
- Provide a personal model for excellence, drive, and success

Can you just imagine what you could accomplish with this type of assistance? The possibilities are endless. However, the efficiency and value of your team depends largely on (1) who you select for your team and (2) how you work with and relate to your team.

First, it is absolutely critical that your Success Team be made up of the right mix of individuals. While this exact mix may differ for each person, there are certain qualities that you should look for. First and foremost, your Success Team should be made up of individuals whose opinions you respect, who are positive, and who are successful themselves. What you are looking for are individuals who can help lead the way, contribute to your success, motivate you to go after it, and provide any direction and assistance you may need. Negative or unsuccessful team members will only suck the energy out of you, model a defeatist attitude, and ultimately point you in the wrong direction. Your best candidates should also be available to support you, be straightforward in their feedback, and have some insight, knowledge, or expertise that is in line with your goals. Now, chances are you won't find one individual that fits all of these criteria, but if the collective make-up of your team as a whole looks like this, then you've probably assembled your best team.

Now that you have enlisted a group of quality individuals for your Success Team, it is equally important to know how to work with them effectively. Here are some of the important things to consider:

- As you are assembling your team, make certain that they understand why you are asking for their support and how you could benefit from their support.

- Try to meet or speak with each team member regularly—whenever is mutually convenient and for whatever time is feasible—to assess your progress and set goals for the next meeting.

- Ask them to keep you accountable for your goals. At the end of each meeting, work together to complete a short list of things to accomplish, leads to follow, or things to learn for the next meeting.

- Respect their time, keep all appointments, and be sure to thank them at the end of every meeting.

- Be prepared and willing to return the favor in the future. Consider what advantages or benefits you have to offer and make them available should your team members ever need assistance themselves.

Assembling and effectively using your Success Team is a fundamental component to personal success. Ultimately, you will benefit from the power and collective expertise of your team working with you to achieve your goals. Pick your team carefully, use it wisely, and reap the rewards!

—*Ross Macpherson, MA, CPRW, CEIP, JCTC, Career Quest*

TIP #14—CREATE YOUR OWN SPACE

Create a comfortable working space devoted exclusively to your search campaign. Realize that a job search is a job, and a job requires an office or, at a minimum, desk space. Rather than trying to manage your search from your dining room table or living room corner, where things will get disrupted, misplaced, and out of order, designate a separate room or area and equip it with the essentials:

- *A PC with Internet access.* In a job search, your computer needs are fairly simple. Although you can use any kind of word processing program to prepare your resume and job search letters, using the industry standard Microsoft Word will promote smooth file transfers with recruiters and employers. You'll also need email software and an Internet browser since the Internet is an essential tool for most job searches. You might also use various PC-based database, contact management, and scheduling programs to store the contact information of your always-growing network and to manage your schedule and task lists.

- *Telephone.* Make sure you have a good message-taking system, whether a separate machine or a voice-mail service. If family members answer your phone, coach them in how to respond and how to take good messages. Also consider adding a fax machine or e-fax capability.

- *High-quality resume paper.* While you might send your resume most frequently via email, at times you'll still need to print good copies—to bring along on interviews, hand out at networking meetings, or use in a traditional paper-mail campaign to target companies. Purchase a supply of good paper with matching envelopes so you're prepared for these occasions. Resume paper can be purchased at most office supply stores and comes in a variety of tasteful colors, weights, and finishes.

- *Mailing supplies.* Have on hand postage stamps, mailing labels, 9 × 12 envelopes, sealing tape, and so forth, for simplifying the administrative tasks of your job search.

To effectively control and manage your job search, think about your needs and stock up beforehand. Manage your job search as you would a business, with a commitment to efficiency and organization.

—*Louise Kursmark, CPRW, JCTC, CEIP, CCM,*
Best Impression Career Services Inc.

TIP #15—GET A SEPARATE PHONE LINE

Although getting a separate phone line (your "job search line") may seem like a minor consideration when you're out of work and worried about where you'll find your next job, it is *not* a minor consideration. If you're looking for a professional position, you must conduct a professional job search, and your ability to communicate on a professional level is vital. Consider the following:

Have you ever called a business associate at home and gotten a small child on the phone who wanted to talk, couldn't find mommy or daddy, or didn't understand what you wanted? What about calling when the phone is answered by a non-English-speaking person (assuming you're calling someone in an English-speaking country)? You try to explain to the person answering the phone that you'd like to speak with Mr. Smith, but to no avail. She simply does not understand you.

If this happens, what do you do? You can struggle on the phone in hopes that you'll be put through to the person you wish to speak to, you can hang up and try back at another time, or you can just give up and never call back. It can be a frustrating situation for the caller and can leave a bad taste in his mouth. If he can't even get you on the phone, how in the world is he ever going to work with you? Instantly, you're categorized as "high maintenance," and people generally do not want to hire individuals who require so much effort.

Don't let that happen to you! A professional job search requires that your phone be answered professionally, either by a real person or voice mail. People are impatient. They will not spend time on the phone encouraging your child to get you or trying to communicate with someone they can't understand. They'll simply give up and call the next applicant; you'll be left out in the cold.

—Author's tip

TIP #16—BUILD A CONTACT DATABASE

Whether you're actively engaged in a job search or simply working to maintain your network of contacts in the event that you may need them in the future, it is vital that you develop an efficient system by which to manage all this information. If not, several things will happen:

- You'll lose a phone message with a new contact's name and number.
- You'll misplace an email address that you need immediately.
- You'll forget to follow up with a recruiter you promised to call regarding a specific position.
- You'll get frustrated with the entire process.

Even worse, you may lose out on a great new opportunity.

Take control and don't let this happen to you. Trying to live by the "Post-It note and scraps of paper" system of organization will not do (although it is one of my personal favorites!). I guarantee you'll get lost in the process. No matter how efficient and on top of things you are, something will fall through the cracks.

Avoiding these pitfalls is easy. Just do one of two things:

1. Set-up a database management system on your PC. If you're not an experienced database user, consider ACT, a user-

friendly program that you'll be able to master quickly. If you have some database experience, consider Microsoft Access for a more sophisticated program with many more options. Take it even one step further and set up a PC-based appointment calendar. The more you automate, the better. It will allow you to manage your search campaign more efficiently while ensuring that you don't miss, forget, or lose anything.

2. Read Tip #5 in this book where I discuss the importance of PC proficiency in today's competitive job market. However, if you're not PC literate, it won't happen overnight, and you'll still need a system to manage your contact information. Here's an easy-to-manage system for you:

    Use a combination of index cards and a notebook. Make an index card for each and every contact. Be sure to use the 4 × 6 cards to give yourself plenty of room for notes. Take all the positive responses you receive that require follow-up action—ranging from a callback in two months to an interview tomorrow—and make a full page for each in your notebook. Then use your notebook to track all subsequent information, interviews, communications, follow-ups, and offers.

Organization and efficiency are the cornerstone of any successful venture, including your search campaign.

—*Author's tip*

TIP #17—STICK TO A SCHEDULE

In preparing to launch your job search, develop a daily schedule to guide your campaign. You'll find that a preplanned schedule will make you more focused, more productive, and more prepared to respond quickly to new opportunities.

Your schedule will depend greatly on the time you have available for your campaign. If you are unemployed, of course, you can devote full time to your job search. But if you're juggling a job with a job search, your time will be more limited, and a schedule is even more important to keep you on track.

Consider the typical activities involved in a job search, and schedule fixed times of day when you'll attack those activities. For instance, you might devote an early-morning hour to responding to job postings and want ads, then pick up the phone at 8 a.m. to start making networking calls. Or perhaps your lunch hour is the best time to be on the phone with potential employers, while your evenings are devoted to activities that don't require you to talk to people while they're working. Whatever you decide, develop a formal schedule and commit yourself to it. You'll have much greater control over your campaign and its success and will be more productive because you're devoting fixed times each day to different aspects of your search.

Obviously, you will need to be flexible in accommodating the schedules of employers, recruiters, network contacts, and others. Interviews always come first, no matter the time of day! Inflexibility leads to lost opportunities, so bend the rules as necessary.

—Louise Kursmark, CPRW, JCTC, CEIP, CCM,
Best Impression Career Services, Inc.

TIP #18—DESIGNING YOUR ROAD MAP TO CAREER SUCCESS

Planning and goal setting are the keys to success in every aspect of your life, including your career. Numerous studies have concluded that those with definite goals and a plan for attaining their goals achieve a higher level of success. Career plans that are assigned definite timelines and committed to paper will ensure your road map to career success.

Dreams and goals are frequently confused. Dreaming is where goals originate, but you must clarify your dreams, identify the steps involved in their attainment, and assign a timeline to transition those dreams into goals. Saying your goal is to become an attorney and to earn $250,000 per year is not enough. You must establish specific tasks and timelines associated with your goal or it is no more than a dream and unlikely to come to fruition. Consider this simple example: If you decide to host a cookout for your friends, you develop a list of things to do and a timeline to ensure each step is completed by the date of the event. You establish a date and time, determine how much you want to spend, invite your friends, select a menu, check supplies, purchase food and drinks, mow the lawn, set up the lawn furniture, get out the grill, prepare the food, decide what you will do if it rains, and so on. As you can see, even a simple goal may have numerous steps involved, many of which need to be executed in some form of sequence. First you set a goal to host a cookout; then you sequentially plan all of the steps.

Let's suppose that your career goal is to work with people. You may consult your career coach and she will ask you to tell her more, but you can't. All you know is that you want to work with people because you're a "people person." Thus far, this is a dream. It is not a goal because it is not specific. That description could fit many occupations including medicine and nursing, retail management, sales, customer service, education and training, financial planning, insurance, public speaking, hotel management, association management, event management, hair styling, massage therapy, and numerous others. So, before you can establish your career goals, you need to clarify in what capacity you would like to work with people. You will need to identify what knowledge, skills, and natural talents you have, what skills and knowledge you will need to develop, what types of working environments you enjoy most, and what types of organizations coincide with your values. Until you crystallize your dreams, you cannot set realistic goals, plan your career, or achieve success.

Establishing your career goals will involve both short- and long-term planning. If you do not know all of the steps involved in reaching your goal, then your first step will to be to research your specific career objectives and take notes about each step so that you can establish a clear-cut timeline. You may also need to develop financial goals to support your career goals. For example, if you want to go to law school and you're not lucky enough to have someone who will pay your tuition, you'll need to research and develop a plan to fund your education. By breaking down your major goal into specific activities, it becomes more realistic and attainable.

Here's a plan of action. Write your daily, weekly, and monthly goals in your daily planner and check each one off as it is completed. These little successes will begin to develop an energy and momentum all their own, and you'll become focused on attaining your long-term goals which may have initially seemed overwhelming. Every time you're faced with making a decision during the day, ask yourself this question, "Will this action move me toward my goal or away from my goal?" If the answer is "toward my goal," then you've made the right decision. Conversely, if the answer is "away from my goal," you know you've got to make a course correction. It is important to re-member that your goals may change and that's okay. Update and rewrite your goals knowing that it is better to have a plan than to just react to circumstances and drift aimlessly through life.

If you have never thought it possible to design your life and career, you may have difficulty initially identifying goals for yourself. You may need to start small and build on the concept. Try writing down five simple activities you want to complete by next week—activities that you've been wanting to complete for some time, but just don't seem to get around to doing. Be specific and include the day, month, and year you expect to complete the activity. Once your first five activities are complete, write down 10 activities you want to complete the fol-lowing week. In the third week, include an activity involving several steps to be completed over a one- or two-month period. This building process develops a sense of self-control and accomplishment. Once you begin to realize the power of planning your activities to achieve short-term goals, you will become motivated to plan long-term goals for all areas of your life.

Review your goals often and visualize yourself having completed each goal. Create a movie in your mind. What will your completed goal feel like, look like, smell like, and sound like? Each night when you go to bed, run your movie. Be sure to see yourself in the movie. Notice how happy you are and how good you feel. This process will start both your subconscious and conscious mind working toward your goal and attract opportunities to you like a magnet.

—Beverly Harvey, CPRW, JCTC, CCM, Beverly Harvey Resume
& Career Services

TIP #19—KNOW WHAT YOU'RE HARD-WIRED TO DO

When you've lost your job or the economy is hitting a downturn, there is a temptation to grab whatever you can get or sell yourself to match whatever a job requires. But if you've talked your way into something which doesn't fit you, you will likely be more vulnerable when there are more layoffs. Yes, it helps to find out what's "out there" when job-hunting, but first find out what's "in there"—what's inside you.

Aptitude testing is the only way to know for sure what you are hard-wired to do—what your natural abilities are. Research has shown that people who work in alignment with their innate talents are more satisfied, productive, and likely to be retained in their job, and better able to market themselves when they can articulate these strengths.

What differentiates aptitude testing from other types of career testing? Most career tests rely on what you report about your personality, interests, skills, or values—all important pieces of the career puzzle, but the results are not always on target or include new information about yourself. However, aptitude testing is based on how you actually perform on specific tasks or problems. This testing reveals strengths that may never have come to light in work or school. It doesn't depend on education or experience. It can tell you what is a natural role or work environment for you, what your problem-solving and decision-making style is, how you communicate most easily, and how you assimilate new information.

For example, on one test you see seven pictures, three of which have something in common. You might see a flashlight, book, bird, calendar, shoe, ice cubes, and a deck of playing cards. The three items with something in common are the book, the calendar, and the playing cards because they are all made out of paper. You would have very little time to find the right answer. People who easily see the answers in a series of these problems have a strong ability seemingly to pull answers out of the air. This is a "right brain," inductive, problem-solving ability since it doesn't use logical, step-by-step reasoning ability. A person who is strong in this ability may find it easier to solve a problem than to explain how they solved it. That person would love being in a job where she can solve problems all day long. She loves challenges and puzzles. People who are strong in this ability often struggle with being bored in situations where they have to do things repetitively or follow up on details.

How a person performs on this test is a good indicator of the pace they would enjoy at work. Someone with a very strong score in this ability would thrive in a troubleshooting role which is almost chaotic, such as an emergency room physician. Someone with a low score might prefer a more stable and predictable work environment. Communication style is also strongly influenced by this ability. The person with the high score is quick, incisive and likes to "cut to the chase." Sometimes he or she may seem impatient or critical of others who are not up to the pace. Conversely, those with lower scores are often better at listening to others, processing and gathering information, and implementing changes.

In aptitude testing you look for patterns of abilities. A person who is strong in both right and left brain problem solving has the ideal consultant ability profile, such as a lawyer. She can quickly grasp the solution to a problem using the ability just described, but also draws on another ability that uses logic to explain her answer to others. If, in addition, she were strong in three-dimensional problem solving, she might enjoy work as a consulting engineer. How she scores on word association tests would reveal whether her natural style is more of a team player or a specialist.

Knowing your most natural style helps you understand what jobs will fully use your strengths and be most satisfying to you. You will know what tasks may be more stressful and how to plan accordingly. People who have had aptitude testing almost always say they wish they could have had this information at an earlier point in their career or education, realizing that they would have saved a lot of time in figuring out what they really enjoy and do best.

—Ann Brody, M.S.W., Career Solutions, Inc.

TIP #20—KNOW YOUR DRIVING FORCE

Unfortunately, the most common approach that job seekers use when starting a full-fledged search is to concentrate on updating their resumes. While the tools of your search (resumes and cover letters) are extremely important, nothing can replace the self-assessment process as a way to build motivation and self-knowledge. The candidate who knows where he wants to go will have the greater chance of getting there, while the "resume first" scenario remains analogous to embarking on a business venture with a brochure rather than a business plan.

Your assessment should lead you to an understanding of what drives you—your motivated skills. These are the skills that clearly define your passion or purpose for working, such as using new technology to improve production, developing new uses for an existing product, or researching historical social trends to identify their impact on today's society. Your motivated skills should answer these questions: What do you consider fun to do? What activities bring you enjoyment? What type of environment do you want to operate in? Where are you the most productive?

Creating a "driving force" statement that evolves from your assessment work adds tremendous impact to your presentation. This simple but dynamic one- or two-sentence statement, which starts with a bold "I," articulates what you want to accomplish for the organization. Your ability to deliver this statement with passion in your voice is what will separate you from your competition. One senior marketing manager who was ready to start a search campaign felt the strength in his presentation when he communicated his driving force, "I want to take new technologies to market." Of course, his resume went on to substantiate his marketable skills and experience needed to accomplish this mission.

The successful job seeker understands the nature of the work he is looking for and is able to articulate those requirements. A person will only be able to get to their end destination by knowing where he wants to go. Your self-assessment work is the primary component of that endeavor. It puts you in control of your job search and separates you from the other applicants.

—Vivian Belen, NCRW, CPRW, JCTC,
The Job Search Specialist

TIP #21—WHO ARE YOU AND WHAT DO YOU WANT?

Imagine you are interviewing candidates for a sales position at your company. You ask the first candidate, "What are you looking for?" The candidate answers, "I'd like a challenging position where I can learn and contribute to the growth of the company." This answer implies that you, as the employer, should determine where the candidate will fit within your company.

You probably won't be inclined to do so, especially when the next candidate answers, "I'd like an account management position where I can significantly grow your business as I did when I won five new clients for XYZ Corporation, representing over a million dollars in revenue. My strengths are consultative selling, customer service, and high-impact presentations. On which one would you like me to elaborate?"

Clearly, this candidate has demonstrated that she knows what she wants and why she is qualified. This kind of focus should be at the core of every career marketing communication—your resume, cover letter, career portfolio, and verbal pitch.

So, how do you figure out who you are and what you want in order to create an effective job search campaign? First, you need to take a step back for self-assessment and research. In order to find a satisfying career, it's necessary to collect data on yourself (inner world) and the world of work (outer world), and then analyze the relationships and themes that emerge between the two. Self-assessment involves understanding your interests, skills, values, and personality/style. Conducting career research involves gathering information on occupations and companies that seem interesting to you and finding out the skills needed, problems to be solved, training required, and where it can be obtained.

There are many resources for career self-assessment. For guidance, you may choose to work with a career coach or counselor who is trained in assessment. Typing "career self-assessment" into your favorite Internet search engine will yield a variety of online options. There are many helpful books on this topic including the classic by Barbara Sher, *I Could Do Anything if I Only Knew What It Was: How to Discover What You Really Want and How to Get It*. Realize that there are no magic answers; no single tool will tell you what you should do. However, when you complete this process, you will be able to make these life-altering decisions based on solid information instead of choosing a career because it just "seems right" or is convenient at the time. Since we spend most of our waking hours at work, it's smart to make an investment in finding something rewarding.

Once armed with information about your skills, values, work style, and possible fields, you'll want to choose a standout career option to research in depth. Begin with researching occupations; then narrow your focus to industries, companies, and decision makers. The best way to conduct research is to use a variety of sources. Start by going to your local library and enlisting help from the reference librarian. Your college or university may also have a career library that you can use as a student or alumni. The Internet has a variety of resources including:

- The Riley Guide to using the Internet for research to support your job search: *www.rileyguide.com/jsresearch.html*
- Occupational Outlook Handbook: *www.bls.gov/oco*
- America's Career InfoNet: *www.acinet.org*
- Company and industry information: *www.hoovers.com* or *www. vault.com*
- Free and subscription-based access to SEC (Securities & Exchange Commission) documents for more than 10,000 public companies: *www.Edgar-Online.com*
- Latest news on a company or industry: *www.PRNewswire.com*
- Salary information: *www.salary.com* or *http://jobstar.org/tools/salary/ negostrt.htm*

Also it's critical to get out and talk to people in the career that you are thinking about pursuing (a.k.a. field research or networking). You may arrange to do job shadowing which involves following someone around for a day to walk in his shoes. Sources for finding the right contacts are:

- Referrals from colleagues and friends
- The alumni or career development office of your educational institution (many have lists of alumni who are willing to talk to people about their career)
- Members of professional associations (consult the *Encyclopedia of Associations*, a directory of 18,000+ professional associations)

Be sure to tell your contacts that you are not looking for a job. Instead, you are seeking advice, information, referrals, and feedback. Set up 20- to 30-minute meetings (face to face is best). An informal chat over lunch or coffee might be more comfortable. Remember that you are in control of these meetings, so you'll want to have a list of questions, and be prepared with research about the organization/field in which the people you'll be interviewing are engaged. Find out:

- How they got into this field
- What a typical day consists of
- What the challenges are
- Where the opportunities are
- What they find rewarding about this work
- What the typical salary range is
- What the industry trends, current demand, and growth potential are
- What the most important professional skills and experience are when hiring people in this line of work
- What industry publications they read and professional associations they belong to
- What suggestions they have for you
- Who else you might talk to

People like to help when you are genuine. It's important to stick to the agreed length of the meeting, send thank-you notes, and follow up with your contacts to let them know the results of their advice and referrals.

After you have researched your career target and feel that it's appropriate for you, go back and take a look at how consistent it is with your skills, values, interests, and style. If you can defend why you should pursue a specific position, then you are ready to write a focused resume and cover letter, prepare for interviews, and launch your job search campaign.

Having done your homework, you'll be able to clearly articulate in your interviews why you are there and what you can contribute. You'll be able to show the hiring manager that you are the round peg that will fit in the round hole. If you know that they need XYZ, then you can convince them that you are XYZ. More importantly, you'll distinguish yourself from a majority of your competition who aren't nearly as well prepared as you.

—Kirsten Dixson, JCTC, CPRW, CEIP, New Leaf
Career Solutions

TIP #22—PACK IT UP AND MOVE IT

Whether you like it or not, it may be that employment opportunities are quite limited in the area in which you are currently living. It may also be that your family and lifelong friends are there. However, to secure the kind and quality of job you are seeking, you may have to move. It's that simple. You may not like it, your family may not like it, but there are areas throughout the United States where jobs are plentiful, and you may need to put yourself there physically in order to take advantage of those opportunities.

What should you consider? Cost of living, housing, weather, sports, cultural and religious groups, schools, employment opportunities for your spouse, and cost of traveling to visit family and friends, are just a few of the things you'll want to investigate. Depending on the availability of qualified candidates within their area, some companies may be willing to pay your travel expenses to interview with them; others will not. Some companies may even pay for relocation; others will not.

There are numerous resources available on the Internet to help you identify and research possible employment opportunities in other areas of the country. Online relocation sites can provide you with information such as employment statistics, industry information, economic growth indicators, and cost-of-living calculations to compare your current cost of living to the area you are considering. Additional sources of information include your targeted city's local newspapers and business magazines, "job bank" publications, professional associations, libraries, and bookstores. You might also contact the local Chamber of Commerce for listings of major employers and industries in the area.

Relocation can also be viewed as a temporary solution in which you can plan to return to your city of choice when the opportunity arrives. If you are unwilling to relocate, you may want to consider changing occupations and/or acquiring new skills that match the types of positions available locally. Or, if you have the qualifications, drive, and financial resources, consider launching your own entrepreneurial venture, business, or consulting practice that will allow you to live anywhere you choose.

—Karen Wrigley, CPRW, JCTC, AMW Career
& Resume Services

TIP #23—OPEN A WINDOW

Whenever NASA launches a space mission, it always establishes a "window," a period in the future when it believes conditions will be optimum for the mission's takeoff. By analogy, anyone thinking of launching a job campaign in a distant city should also consider "opening a window" (choosing a time to go to that city to seek employment). Going to another location to look for a new position can cost time and money. Nevertheless, properly done, it can shorten your job search. Remember that since you are in direct competition with job seekers already in that location, extra effort is required on your part to overcome their geographical advantage. Here's how:

First, choose a "window" four to six weeks in the future and make tentative travel plans. This should be far enough in advance to give you time to write and call prospective employers to make sure that their calendars are still open by the time you get there.

Second, write to decision makers at companies of interest and include a copy of your resume. Explain that you intend to relocate to their area in the near future and that you believe your background and skills should be of interest to them and their colleagues. Cite the dates that you will be in their area, and then add that you will be calling them soon to see if you can meet with them during that time. (*Hint:* Add in a postscript that even if they have no openings, you would still appreciate a few minutes of their time to get their perspective on the job market in that city/region. Thus, you will not only gain some useful information, but build them into your network for later use.)

Write similar letters to local recruiters, letting them know that you will be available for interviews with any of their clients at that time or, if need be, at another time. Do not forget to respond to advertisements as well, once again explaining when you will be available for interviews.

Third, follow up with phone calls. If you cannot reach prospective employers at once, explain to their secretaries or staff members that you are calling long distance and would appreciate knowing the best time to call back. Ask them to let their boss know that you will be calling at that time.

If, when you do reach your target, you are told they have no openings, remember to press for an information interview. Decision makers, if approached tactfully, can afford you a wealth of useful information even if they are not in a position to offer you a job. To learn about information interviews, read Tip #70 in Chapter 6.

Finally, if after a concerted effort you have not generated enough interviews to make your trip worthwhile, then create a new "window" a bit further in the future, reschedule meetings you have already arranged, and start your campaign anew.

The IRS generally considers job-hunting costs, whether local or long distance, as miscellaneous itemized deductions when you are looking for a new position in the same line of work. This remains true regardless of whether you are now employed and whether you find a new job or not. Such deductions include the costs of preparing, printing, or mailing your resume; career counseling fees; long distance phone calls; or travel, meals, and lodging expenses. Remember that if you meet the IRS time and distance requirements, you may also deduct moving expenses incurred while making a long-distance move to a new job. You may not, however, deduct expenses you incur looking for your first job in a new field regardless of its location.

Making a successful long-distance move is not easy. Realistic goals, careful planning, and dogged persistence should get you to your goals in most cases and a lot faster than it took NASA to get us to the moon!

—*Pierre G. Daunic, Ph.D., CCM, R.L. Stevens & Associates*

TIP #24—GET PROFESSIONAL ASSISTANCE

Career counselors have been a part of the fabric of the employment industry for decades. However, most career counselors have focused on helping individuals resolve work-related issues, intervening in work-related crises, supporting individuals after they've been laid-off, assisting those who are transitioning their careers, or guiding high school and college graduates in identifying their career options. Career counselors are often characterized as crisis managers and problem solvers, a vital component in the employment market, but somewhat limited in their focus.

More recently, the profession of career coaching has evolved and risen to the top ranks of the careers industry. Coaching is generally characterized as broader and more diverse in its service offerings than the traditional career counseling approach. Consider the following services and expertise that a career coach can offer to you:

- Coaches help you closely examine and assess your skills, knowledge, qualifications, and goals so that you have a better understanding of yourself and the value you offer to a prospective employer.

- Coaches help you evaluate the various career paths available to you and educate you about new jobs, industries, professions, and possibilities you may never have considered.

- Coaches help you determine and resolve issues impeding the progress of your job search and your career.

- Coaches guide you in researching and developing a winning job search campaign that uses all of the appropriate job search channels that are right for you (e.g., networking, ad responses, Internet resume postings, email campaigns to recruiters, direct mail campaigns to companies, job lead reports).

- Coaches teach you how to sharpen your interviewing skills so that you will be sure to interview at your peak performance regardless of the interview situation (e.g., phone, in person, panel).

- Coaches teach you how to be a savvy negotiator to ensure that you'll get the best salary and compensation package available to you.

- Coaches stay with you, if you want, providing ongoing career support and guidance even when you're happily and profitably employed. They help resolve work-related problems, negotiate for promotions, design continuing training and development plans, and counsel you relative to your next career move.

Many job seekers are now opting for the additional help offered by career coaches, realizing the value they bring to you in preparing, planning, and conducting a winning job search campaign and helping you achieve lifelong career satisfaction. If you believe a coach would be a benefit to you, be a wise shopper and talk to several coaches before you select one. Just as in other careers, coaches tend to specialize. Some focus on "front-end" coaching (e.g., assessment, planning, crisis management); others focus on "back-end" coaching (e.g., job search, interviewing, salary negotiations). You must find a career coach that offers the services that you need.

Just as critical, you need to find a coach that you like and feel comfortable with. In many instances, you'll be sharing personal information with your coach and you must be able to do so without feeling threatened or uncomfortable. You want a coach who you can trust, who is supportive, who has a personality style that fits comfortably with yours, who you understand, and who you respect. Your coaching relationship may only last a few weeks; for others, it may last for years.

Once you've found a coach that you think is appropriate and will be valuable to you, check him out. Verify his credentials and certifications to be sure that he is well trained and well qualified. Then, ask for references and talk with other job seekers who've used his services. Did the coach deliver as promised? Was he supportive? Did he have innovative ideas and strategies? Was he successful in helping the job seeker find a new opportunity?

To help you identify the "right" career coach to propel your career, visit the websites of these associations to learn about their membership:

- Career Masters Institute: *www.cminstitute.com*
- Career Coach University: *www.careercoachu.com*
- International Coach Federation: *www.coachfederation.org*
- Professional Association of Resume Writers/Career Coaches: *www.parw.com*

> —*Rolande L. LaPointe, CPC, CIPC, CPRW, IJCTC, CCM,*
> *RO-LAN Associates, Inc.*

Career Planning and Preparedness Checklist

Directions: Use the following checklist as a step-by-step tool for career planning and lifelong career management.

Have you . . .

- Started to develop your career plan and job search plan *now*? ☐
- Hired a professional career coach or counselor? ☐
- Overcome (in your mind) any obstacles that may impede your search or career growth? ☐
- Assembled your success team to help guide your career and job search? ☐
- Won the support and assistance of your family, friends, and close colleagues? ☐
- Prepared a detailed list of ALL of your network contacts? ☐
- Established a daily career planning and job search schedule? ☐
- Set up a dedicated work space for your career management needs? ☐
- Obtained a private email address for your search campaign? ☐
- Completed any career assessment or self-assessment instruments? ☐
  Name of Assessment: _____ Date: _____
  Name of Assessment: _____ Date: _____
  Name of Assessment: _____ Date: _____
- Researched "hot" industries and professions that meet your objectives? ☐
- Defined your position goals and objectives? ☐
- Defined your industry goals and objectives? ☐
- Defined your salary/compensation requirements? ☐

- Defined your geographic preferences and evaluated your ability to relocate? ☐
- Written a concise statement of your "career value" for recruiters and employers? ☐
- Identified your top three professional skills most saleable in today's employment market? ☐
- Sought professional assistance to develop a professional resume and cover letter? ☐
- Sought professional assistance to develop other career marketing materials? ☐
- Committed yourself to job search success and lifelong career satisfaction? ☐

CHAPTER 3

Writing Winning Resumes and Cover Letters That Get You Noticed

TIP #25—WRITING TO SELL THE BEST PRODUCT OF ALL—YOU!

You will hear this theme repeated over and over in this publication . . . job search is sales. You have a product to sell—*yourself*—and your challenge is to develop powerful marketing communications that highlight the benefits and value of that product. It is not enough to write a summary of your employment experience (your responsibilities) and your education, then call it a resume. Today's resume is a document that highlights success, achievement, value, and contribution. It is designed to sell, entice a prospective employer, and competitively position you above other candidates.

How can you incorporate marketing concepts into your resume?

* *Understand the "product."* Remember, the product is you. Be sure you're communicating, very clearly, just what the product is. Are you a financial executive/CFO? A sales manager? A systems ana-

lyst? A technical writer? Whatever function you fulfill for a company, be sure it's clear from a quick read of your resume. Employers will *not* take the time to figure it out!

- *Position the product.* Know how you want to be perceived and position yourself with that picture in mind. If you're a technology manager, don't make the mistake of overloading your resume with technical capabilities no matter how strong your technology skills. You'll be perceived as a hands-on "techie" rather than an IT manager. Instead, emphasize your strategic planning and team leadership skills, financial oversight responsibilities, and other higher-level management strengths.

- *Emphasize benefits.* It's an oft-repeated phrase in sales and marketing: "Sell benefits, not features." This is as true in marketing yourself as it is in selling laundry detergent. "Contains RP-7 dynamic cleaning agent" (a feature) doesn't sell as well as "Uses the latest technology to give you whiter whites and brighter colors!" (a benefit). In job search, you must answer the employer's #1 question, *"What's in it for me?"* To an employer, a B.S. in industrial engineering is a feature; a proven record of cutting manufacturing costs through process improvements is a benefit an employer will appreciate and value.

- *Add credibility with specific, measurable results.* If you state you have "a proven record of cutting manufacturing costs," be sure to support this statement with specific examples of what you did and the savings it yielded (dollar amounts or percentages).

If your resume and cover letter don't market you appropriately, you'll never get the chance to prove your value in an interview. Your marketing documents should grab the reader's attention, convey measurable benefits, and make you look like a highly qualified, proven performer for exactly the type of job you're interested in.

—Louise Kursmark, CPRW, JCTC, CEIP, CCM, Best
Impression Career Services, Inc.

TIP #26—THERE ARE NO RULES

There are no rules for resume writing. There is no single template or predefined set of instructions. What you do—in the writing and the design of your resume—is entirely up to you. And that is what makes resume writing such a challenge!

To make things easier for you, here's a quick overview of what sections you must, should, and may include in your resume:

Must Include:

*   Experience (specifically, names of companies, job titles, and dates of employment). There are exceptions to including dates if you are 50 years of age or older. See Tip #34 in this chapter for information.

*   Education (unless you have no high school degree or no college).

The trick is to start your resume with the information that is most supportive of your current career goals. What does that mean? If you're a recent college graduate, most likely your education is your #1 selling point. Include that information first; then follow with your experience. Conversely, if you are a working professional, generally your experience will be your #1 selling point, with education at the end of your resume.

Should Include:

*   Career Summary (at the top of your resume)—may also be called professional qualifications, technical qualifications, career profile, executive profile, summary of skills, or career achievements. This is the section that will catch your reader's interest because you've displayed your most notable skills and accomplishments for immediate review. This is the section that allows you to immediately communicate, "This is who I am."

May Include (if relevant to your career):

Publications	Professional Affiliations
Public Speaking	Civic Affiliations

Honors & Awards

Teaching Experience

Technology Skills

Volunteer Experience

Foreign Language Skills

International Experience

Licenses & Credentials

Personal Profile

—Author's tip

TIP #27—THE ONE-PAGE RULE

All too many job seekers develop their resumes based on the unwritten "one-page rule," an unknown rule, developed by an unknown person for some unknown reason. In fact, it's in an unknown source since no one has ever seen it. Well, forget it! There is no "one-page rule."

If you are a recent college graduate or a young professional, chances are that your resume will comfortably fit on one page. That's great. However, even for younger adults, that won't always be the case. It may be that you've had a great deal of relevant work experience or unique educational opportunities. It may be that you've volunteered abroad, have an interesting competitive sports background, or are an accomplished stage performer, all of which are things you would certainly want to include on your resume even if they weren't directly relevant to your current career goals. They're interesting, communicate certain things about you and your character, and are great points for discussion during an interview. What's more, people want to hire interesting, well-rounded individuals who bring a diversity of skills and experiences to their organizations.

If you are a professional with 5+ years of experience, a manager or an executive, chances are likely that you won't be able to include everything that is important on just one page. It's okay! Two-page resumes are just as acceptable as one-pagers and are often preferred for higher-level positions when it's necessary to provide more information. The objective of your resume is to "sell" yourself, highlight your achievements and successes, detail your employment experience, and "tempt" a prospective employer. Whether it's one page or two is totally incidental to that process.

Finally, there are even certain professions (e.g., academia, health care, research, science) where resumes can go on for pages and pages, with lengthy lists of publications, public speaking engagements, teaching experiences, board appointments, professional affiliations, licenses, credentials, training, and more. A resume such as this is referred to as a curriculum vitae (CV) and is characterized by lists of information that would never be included on a "traditional" business resume.

—Author's tip

TIP #28—SELECT THE RESUME STYLE THAT'S RIGHT FOR YOU

When writing your resume, you must select from one of three basic resume styles—chronological, functional, or combination. Each style serves a different purpose and has a different focus. Carefully review each of the following and select the one that will work best for you. You should make that decision based on your past experience and, more importantly, on your current career objectives.

- Chronological resumes are focused on the strength of your work experience, and are the most typical and most widely accepted style. They are written in what is referred to as reverse chronology, starting with your most recent position and working your way back in time. When writing your job descriptions, you want to accomplish two things. First, you must provide a good description of the company and your responsibilities in general. Second, you follow with the highlights—your achievements, special projects, awards, contributions, and more.

See pages 52–53 for an example of a chronological resume.

- Functional resumes are focused on the strength of your specific skills and qualifications. This style of resume is much less frequently used and generally only recommended when your past work history is *not* in line with your current career objectives. When you write a functional resume, you want to pull out the highlights of your career—your skills, achievements, experiences, projects, and more—that are related to your current career objectives and not what you did in the past. You then take that information and present it at the beginning of your resume, in as much detail as necessary and then just briefly list your work experience at the end.

See page 54 for an example of a functional resume.

- Combination resumes are just that—a combination of the best features of both the chronological and functional resume styles. Combinations begin with a strong summary at the beginning of the resume, focusing on your most significant skills, qualifications, and achievements, just as a functional resume does. You then follow that with your chronological work experience, written with good strong descriptions of overall responsibilities and highlights of your achievements. Combination resumes work to everyone's advantage—the job seeker and the employer. The job seeker is able to sell the success of all he has accomplished; the employer clearly "sees" the job seeker's achievements in addition to his strong chronological work history.

See pages 55–57 for an example of a combination resume.

—Author's tip

LINDA SORENSON
Architectural Designer

PROFESSIONAL EXPERIENCE

Drafter / Designer
Design / build
Commercial interior design
Residential & commercial
design

Linda Sorenson Designs, London, England, UK
INDEPENDENT DESIGN CONSULTANT   1999 - Present
Projects included law offices, dental offices and residences.

- Co-designed a 3,000 square foot restoration of a 1650 residence.
- Designed complete furnishings for an 11-room home.

Gained a reputation for sensitive restoration of period properties.

Academic Credentials
BA Honors Interior and
Spatial Design

London Building Interiors, London, England, UK
DESIGN COORDINATOR / HEAD DESIGNER   1995 - 1999

- Designed a model office showcasing the company's products and services.
- Established a library of design resources and materials, successfully attracting a customer base of sales and design professionals.
- Recruited, selected and trained design personnel.
- Coordinated and evaluated work plans and supervised projects on-site.

Exceeded sales goals and closed repeat business.

Design Skills
Schematics
Contract drawings
Materials research
Specifications
Freehand drawing
Presentation boards/models

Architectural Concepts, Inc., London, England, UK
SENIOR DESIGNER   1992 - 1995
Rapid promotion to Senior Designer in an architectural office. Designed and managed million dollar bank projects. Worked on design/build projects, floor plans and ATMs.

- *Marketing:* Performed needs assessments, designed work flow systems, prepared and presented schematics, and made formal presentations. Prepared bid packages to be sent out to contractors and sub-contractors. Handled price negotiations.
- *Visual Presentations:* Produced design boards showing detailed millwork and special finishes. Created full-color sketches in perspective of interior and exterior site plans.
- *Technical:* Specified interior finishing, furnishings and exterior materials. Drafted specifications and full working drawings.

Brought projects in on-time and under budget, every time.
Personally assured quality of workmanship through on-site supervision.
Designed a stage set for the "Bank of the Future," Bristol, England, UK.

Executive Capabilities
Project management
Sales & marketing
Price negotiation
Organizational ability
Delivering projects on-time
under budget

Graves & Thompson, London, England, UK
DESIGN CONSULTANT   1992

- Completed floor plans for a 160-unit condominium project.
- Produced drawings for framing, electrical and HVAC.

Contributed to bringing the project in under cost projections by designing meticulous plans.

Interpersonal Skills
Architect interface
Contractor interface
Customer service

Central Episcopal Hospital, Herefordshire, England, UK
ARCHITECTURAL DRAFTER   1991

- Collaborated with the designer in collecting data and drafting plans.
- Ensured existing drawings conformed with engineering, construction and repair plans.

Facilitated timely completion of projects and minimal disruption to residents by providing accurate design materials and precise instructions to contractors.

Hampstead Road ▪ London, SW3 6LS UK ▪ 011+44-20-7815 6977 ▪ l@sorenson.co.uk

LINDA SORENSON

EDUCATION

Interpersonal Skills
Team player
Public relations
Tact and diplomacy

South Bank University, London, England, UK
Masters Program in Interior Architecture   2000 - Present
Coursework to date: Algebraic Structures I & II; Theory/Forum; CAD 2-D;
Design Studio A1/A2; DataCad II/3D Modeling; Design Studio B; Values; Perspective
Drawing; AutoCad 3-D.

Hereford College of Art and Design, Hereford, England, UK
BA Honors Interior and Spatial Design   1991

Computer Skills
AutoCad 13/14, 3-D
DataCad
Lotus Notes
MS Word
PowerPoint
Excel

Architectural Association School of Architecture, London, England, UK
Coursework: Architectural Design, AutoCad   1996

AFFILIATIONS

Member, Association of Architects and Designers   2000 - Present
Member, Institute of International Business Designers   1991 - Present

References & Portfolio Available Upon Request

Resume Written & Designed By Jean Cummings, A Resume For Today

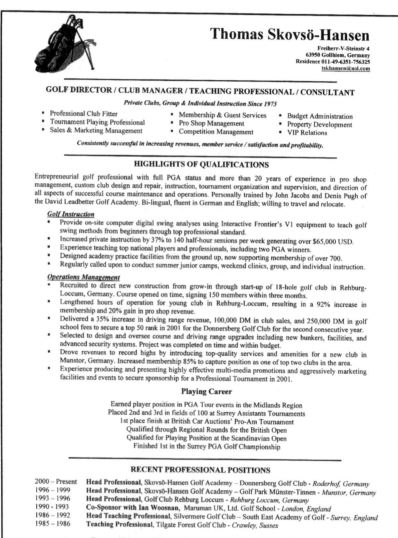

Thomas Skovsö-Hansen

Freiherr-V-Steinstr 4
63950 Gollhiem, Germany
Residence 011-49-6351-756325
tskhansen@aol.com

GOLF DIRECTOR / CLUB MANAGER / TEACHING PROFESSIONAL / CONSULTANT

Private Clubs, Group & Individual Instruction Since 1973

- Professional Club Fitter
- Tournament Playing Professional
- Sales & Marketing Management
- Membership & Guest Services
- Pro Shop Management
- Competition Management
- Budget Administration
- Property Development
- VIP Relations

Consistently successful in increasing revenues, member service / satisfaction and profitability.

HIGHLIGHTS OF QUALIFICATIONS

Entrepreneurial golf professional with full PGA status and more than 20 years of experience in pro shop management, custom club design and repair, instruction, tournament organization and supervision, and direction of all aspects of successful course maintenance and operations. Personally trained by John Jacobs and Denis Pugh of the David Leadbetter Golf Academy. Bi-lingual, fluent in German and English; willing to travel and relocate.

Golf Instruction

- Provide on-site computer digital swing analyses using Interactive Frontier's V1 equipment to teach golf swing methods from beginners through top professional standard.
- Increased private instruction by 37% to 140 half-hour sessions per week generating over $65,000 USD.
- Experience teaching top national players and professionals, including two PGA winners.
- Designed academy practice facilities from the ground up, now supporting membership of over 700.
- Regularly called upon to conduct summer junior camps, weekend clinics, group, and individual instruction.

Operations Management

- Recruited to direct new construction from grow-in through start-up of 18-hole golf club in Rehburg-Loccum, Germany. Course opened on time, signing 150 members within three months.
- Lengthened hours of operation for young club in Rehburg-Loccum, resulting in a 92% increase in membership and 20% gain in pro shop revenue.
- Delivered a 35% increase in driving range revenue, 100,000 DM in club sales, and 250,000 DM in golf school fees to secure a top 50 rank in 2001 for the Donnersberg Golf Club for the second consecutive year.
- Selected to design and oversee course and driving range upgrades including new bunkers, facilities, and advanced security systems. Project was completed on time and within budget.
- Drove revenues to record highs by introducing top-quality services and amenities for a new club in Munstor, Germany. Increased membership 85% to capture position as one of top two clubs in the area.
- Experience producing and presenting highly effective multi-media promotions and aggressively marketing facilities and events to secure sponsorship for a Professional Tournament in 2001.

Playing Career

Earned player position in PGA Tour events in the Midlands Region
Placed 2nd and 3rd in fields of 100 at Surrey Assistants Tournaments
1st place finish at British Car Auctions' Pro-Am Tournament
Qualified through Regional Rounds for the British Open
Qualified for Playing Position at the Scandinavian Open
Finished 1st in the Surrey PGA Golf Championship

RECENT PROFESSIONAL POSITIONS

2000 – Present	**Head Professional**, Skovsö-Hansen Golf Academy – Donnersberg Golf Club - *Roderhof, Germany*
1996 – 1999	**Head Professional**, Skovsö-Hansen Golf Academy – Golf Park Münster-Tinnen - *Munstor, Germany*
1993 – 1996	**Head Professional**, Golf Club Rehburg Loccum - *Rehburg Loccum, Germany*
1990 - 1993	**Co-Sponsor with Ian Woosnan**, Maruman UK, Ltd. Golf School - *London, England*
1986 – 1992	**Head Teaching Professional**, Silvermere Golf Club – South East Academy of Golf - *Surrey, England*
1985 – 1986	**Teaching Professional**, Tilgate Forest Golf Club - *Crawley, Sussex*

Resume Written & Designed By Debbie Ellis, Phoenix Career Group

EDUARDO RENDON

3617 Pinnacle Road
San Diego, CA 95174

(415) 672-6792
edrendon@aol.com

SENIOR HUMAN RESOURCES & ORGANIZATIONAL EFFECTIVENESS EXECUTIVE
US & International Organizations ... High-Growth, Turnaround & Fortune 500

Business Partner to senior operating and leadership executives to guide the development of performance-driven, customer-driven, market-driven organizations. Recognized for innovative leadership and counsel in transitioning under-performing organizations into top producers and guiding other organizations through accelerated growth and global market expansion. Decisive, energetic and focused. Talented team leader, team player and project manager. Fluent in Spanish, German and English.

Strategic HR Leader with expert qualifications in all generalist HR affairs. Particular success in:

• Performance Management Systems	• Quality Improvement Processes	• Change Management
• Process Redesign & Reengineering	• 306-Degree Feedback Systems	• Job Process Design
• Employee Satisfaction & Retention	• Rewards & Incentive Programs	• Self-Directed Teams
• Training, Coaching & Team Building	• Organizational Assessments	• Cycle Time Reductions
• Leadership/Competency Development	• Business & People Strategies	• Process Optimization

ACCOMPLISHMENT HIGHLIGHTS

☑ **International Experience**: Extensive management and consulting experience with companies operating in Central America and U.S. In-depth understanding of regional labor codes. Managed HR programs for expatriates.

☑ **Organizational Development (OD) Initiatives**: Led many large-scale change programs involving change management, organizational redesign, corporate restructuring, and productivity, performance and efficiency improvement. Delivered multi-million dollar cost savings.

☑ **Human Resource Programs**: Instituted 306-degree feedback processes. Designed new HR strategies including new employee orientation programs, rewards and recognition systems, and flextime schedules. Coached corporate executives through leadership and change management initiatives.

☑ **Training & Development**: Trained all levels of staff including executives in one-on-one, small and large group settings. Expert in adult learning principles, instructional design, program organization and experimental learning.

☑ **Management/HR Instruction**: Taught courses in change management, team building, coaching, self-directed team leadership, experimental learning, customer service, group facilitation, training the trainer, leadership development and new business development.

☑ **Executive, Management & Leadership Development**: Designed and implemented Leadership Executive Development Program with Wharton School of Business for business leaders of El Salvador. Currently leading supervisory/management development program for middle managers, incorporating action learning processes.

☑ **Team Building**: Instituted team-based programs for numerous organizations implementing large-scale change or single department initiatives. Marketed brand-name product, TEAMS, in Central America that increased employee satisfaction levels and delivered gains in quality improvement and cost savings for other companies.

☑ **Benefits & Compensation Plans**: Redesigned compensation systems using variable pay system. Restructured salary scales based on competency models creating career ladder for technical employees. Implemented innovative performance-based reward systems minimizing costs of turnover, workers' compensation and low attendance.

PROFESSIONAL EXPERIENCE

Best Services International, San Diego, CA   2000-Present
$7 billion corporation with 12 million customers in more than 40 countries. Named #1 most admired outsourcing company in the world by Fortune Magazine.

ORGANIZATIONAL EFFECTIVENESS DIRECTOR

Recruited to lead large-scale change initiative in Best Service's Hospitality Service Management Division and manage non-clinical health services for two major hospitals in San Diego (through contract with SoCal Healthcare Systems). Implement strategy design, process improvement, human resources systems redesign, coaching, teambuilding and leadership development.

Operate under matrix organization reporting to VP of Integrated Support Services, Regional Organizational Effectiveness Director for the West Region and the Advisory Board including hospital-based COO, VP of Human Resources and VP of Operations for Best Services.

- Restructured seven non-clinical departments into single integrated department, requiring staff downsizing and implementation of new systems and processes. Sustained same service quality levels through transition.
- Instituted integrated service model and organizational effectiveness tools: key focus indicators (balance score card), performance management model, Ready for Healthcare (employee orientation system), We S.E.R.V.E. (customer service program), Feeding the Roots (leadership development), Service Center (call center), continuous value improvement program and service partner selection process.
- Revamped hiring selection process for hospital's Support Service Department including behavioral-based tools for hiring/developing employees, standardization of hiring selection tools and team-based interviews. Retrained hiring managers. Reduced selection process cycle time from 4 weeks to 1 week.
- Ensured 5-year cost savings projected at $2.5 million. Improved employee satisfaction levels by 20%.

Escuela Superior de Economia y Negocios, El Salvador, C.A.   1995-2000
Prestigious, non-profit economic development organization offering OD consulting services for private and government sector, executive training programs and economic research studies through Economic and Business University in Latin America.

ORGANIZATIONAL DEVELOPMENT CONSULTANT

Program manager for undergraduate business and organizational development extension program at University. Professor of Management, New Business Development and Leadership/Teambuilding programs.

Consulted with corporate clients on organizational development initiatives to drive gains in productivity, quality, cost control and employee satisfaction such as process improvement, operational effectiveness, human resources strategies, reengineering, downsizing and self-directed teams. Clients included Xerox, Pizza Hut, Convergence Communications, Cablevisa, Intercontinental Hotel, La Constancia and others.

- **Convergence Communications, Inc.**: Spearheaded new HR initiatives designed to boost OE competency, employee satisfaction, quality and service. Redesigned compensation and performance/evaluation systems. Led company restructuring and downsizing. Reduced overhead expenses by 15% and improved productivity from 73% to 85%. Trained employees to integrate new products and service requirements with no loss of productivity and sustained high levels of service and quality.
- **La Constancia, S.A.**: Guided Central America's largest brewery through a "Whole System Change Process" that increased productivity, improved employee satisfaction and reduced costs over $1 million.
- **Viper, S.A.**: Led strategic planning effort to streamline key operations, reduce cycle times and improve productivity. Repositioned company as a market leader in the pager services industry.
- **Xerox**: Instituted work groups for technical service department that increased employee satisfaction levels from 73% to 94% in a year.

- **Pizza Hut**: Supported launch of HR strategy to increase quality, productivity and employee satisfaction. Trained 100+ managers and employees in change management, team building and coaching. Positioned company as #1 in fast food industry in local market.
- **Cablevisa**: Reorganized largest cable network in El Salvador, facilitating reengineering project to reduce cycle times, increase customer satisfaction, eliminate bottlenecks and reduce overhead costs.
- **Additional assignments** included work with Intercontinental Hotel, Banco Capital, Toyota and others.

Duramas, El Salvador, C.A.   1993-1995
Largest shoe manufacturer and retailer in Central America, producing top brands including Bally, Sebago, Caterpillar and Hush Puppies. Division of ADOC.

ORGANIZATIONAL DEVELOPMENT MANAGER

Spearheaded process reengineering initiative. Facilitated, coordinated, integrated and motivated workforce to form self-directed work teams and implement change initiatives that reduced cycle times and improved quality and productivity.

- Reduced shoe manufacturing costs from $22 to $19.

General Electric, Moorestown, NJ & Louisville, KY   1991-1993

MASTER IN MANUFACTURING PROGRAM MEMBER

Completed 500+ hours of graduate-level coursework and four manufacturing work assignments in high-volume manufacturing of consumer products and low-volume manufacturing for government contracts. Focused on quality, information systems, industrial engineering, production and supervision. Assignments included:

- **Quality Leader, GE Aerospace**. Managed 1st and 2nd shift quality team (70 employees) inspecting five major components. Motivated workforce to meet business goals. Fostered communication between functional groups. Addressed customer concerns with proactive action. Improved process yields 15%.
- **Industrial Engineer, GE Aerospace**. Led process measurement initiative by GE-IUE union to reduce cycle time and established type-2 engineering rates for work center. Supported Characteristic Verification Process CVP, a quality improvement effort, during pilot runs in two work centers. Reduced cycle time by 10%.
- **Production Engineer, GE Appliances**. Supported production design in shop operations, initiating changes through idea generation and feasibility/evaluation testing. Managed quality improvement projects, enhanced product production, reduced service call rates and material cost take-outs. Helped to implement self-directed work teams by leading steering committee to develop team guidelines. Oversaw process improvement project to reduce cracked liners. Captured total cost savings of $200,000+.
- **Systems Support Engineer, GE Appliances**. Key implementation team member for Material Scheduling & Quick Response Information system that included billing, inventory control, material flow, parts scheduling and engineering management.

EDUCATION

M.A., Organizational Design & Effectiveness, UCLA, 2000
Executive Certificate Program in Business Administration, University of Barcelona, Spain, 1995
Master in Manufacturing Management, GE Leadership Executive Development, 1993
B.S., Mechanical Engineering, Marquette University, 1991

AFFILIATIONS

Organizational Development Network ▪ Society for Human Resource Management
Competitiveness Network for El Salvador ▪ Funding member of ROTARY International of Ciudad Merliott

Resume Written & Designed By Lynn Andenoro, My Career Resource

TIP #29—OBJECTIVES MAY BE OBSOLETE

Does your resume lead off with an objective statement that clearly sets forth your target position? "Objective: A sales/account management position with an industry leader in the medical equipment field."

Or, to cover many bases, did you write a general purpose objective that employers can interpret to fit their hiring needs? "Seeking a challenging position with opportunity for advancement, where proven skills will be used and efforts rewarded."

Either example is *not* the best way to begin your resume. A focused objective statement, such as the first example, can certainly help an employer pinpoint your area of expertise, but in both cases the objective says far more about what you want than what you have to offer. Keep in mind, an employer's underlying question in every hiring campaign is "What can you do for me?" An objective does not answer that question.

A section called Career Summary, Experience Profile, or Qualifications Brief is a much more effective way to introduce yourself and begin your resume. A powerful summary tells employers the key advantages you offer: your experience, accomplishments, skills, knowledge, and track record of performance. In your summary, you can highlight the most impressive things about your background from the point of view of an employer. A powerful summary "paints a picture" of who you are and what you have to offer and will clearly position you for the type and level of position you are seeking. In other words, it communicates the same (or more) information as an objective but does so in an employer-centered way.

Consider this sample Career Summary for the medical salesperson whose objective appears above:

Medical Sales Professional with unbroken record of revenue growth and territory expansion.

- Eight years' experience selling capital medical equipment with Siemens and Mallinckrodt

- Twice built new territories from the ground up to top 10 percent nationally
- Grew territory revenue 47 percent through effective consultative selling
- Nursing background and in-depth understanding of hospital purchasing procedures

A summary communicates more meaningful information than an objective. It motivates employers to read the rest of your resume and gives many reasons for them to call you for an interview. A powerful summary will give your resume a competitive advantage in the employment marketplace.

—Louise Kursmark, CPRW, JCTC, CEIP, CCM, Best
Impression Career Services, Inc.

TIP #30—WRITE IN THE FIRST PERSON

Write your resume and your cover letters in the first person (dropping the word *I*), not the third person. If you write in the first person, you assume ownership of the task, the achievement, or the project. When you write in the third person, it's as if someone else is taking responsibility for what you did.

Compare these two examples:

First Person: Negotiated $2.2 million sales contract with General Electric.

Third Person: Mrs. Riley negotiated a $2.2 million sales contract with General Electric.

See the difference? The first person is active; the third person is passive.

Here's another example:

First Person: Developed and implemented a new record-keeping system that reduced errors 12 percent.

Third Person: Ms. Radcliffe developed and implemented a new record-keeping system that reduced errors 12 percent.

To give your resume the energy and power it needs, you must use the active tone.

—Author's tip

TIP #31—A Few Good Words

The prime key to job search success is a great resume tailored specifically for you and your career. Using the power of the written word and combining it with research enables you to prepare a well-written, eye-catching document. This type of writing differs from general writing, including stories, essays, and commentaries, and falls into the realm of technical writing. Concise sentences using adjectives, industry key words, and as few words as possible can make a powerful statement.

When women meet, they kiss one another. Men usually greet each other with a handshake and ask "What's the good word?" What a wonderful way to start a conversation. Our accomplishments with words are the result of having the ability to speak and write as a means of communication.

In resume writing, the power of the "good word" is what enables you to prepare a public relations document about yourself. New words, new meanings, and other pertinent facts can help you transform ordinary writing into an outstanding resume.

Words are tools that describe your talents, abilities, and accomplishments. It doesn't matter if the words are big or little as long as you are able to paint a picture about yourself depicting what you would like the reader to know. A reader will scan a resume in two to three seconds. Consequently, you should write clearly and to the point. In his book, *Think Outside the Box: The Most Trite, Generic, Hokey, Overused, Cliched or Unmotivating Motivational Slogans,* Dr. James A. Tompkins writes "Remember, we can't spell SUCCESS without U."

There are a variety of sources which you can use to find great words. Dictionaries, synonym finders or thesauri are great reference books to use for locating precise and expressive words. In addition, there are newspapers, magazines, books, and more, all excellent resources to find new words and understand their usage. Your challenge is to find those words, use them correctly, and demonstrate your communications proficiency!

Although many people study English in high school and college, they are not adept at writing clearly. As a result, there are times when people have been hired primarily because of their writing skills. They demonstrated, through their resume and cover letter, that they were able to write intelligent, clear, and readable business documents. That, in and of itself, is a great asset for any employer.

Whenever you're writing job search materials—resumes, cover letters, thank-you letters, and more—remind yourself that prospective employers are going to use those documents to gauge the overall quality of your writing skills. Be sure to select and use your words wisely, write with style and flair, and concisely communicate your key points. Follow through with those same concepts when demonstrating your verbal communication skills in an interview and you're bound to win. Be confident that your ability to use words wisely will give you a remarkable advantage over your competition.

—*Anne Kramer, CPRW, Alpha Bits*

TIP #32—Use Key Words to Sell

Ten years ago, no one had even heard of key words, yet they're nothing new. Previously known as buzz words, key words are nouns and nouns phrases that are specific to a particular industry or profession. Here are a few examples of key words and key word phrases for specific professions:

Teaching: curriculum development, instructional methods, classroom management, learner motivation, testing, textbook review, teacher training, multimedia resources, student activities

Customer service: customer relationship management, customer care, order processing, order fulfillment, telemarketing, telesales, key account management, problem resolution

Transportation: driver leasing, warehousing, distribution, asset management, inventory control, dedicated logistics, fleet management, import/export operations

Key words have two vital purposes in your job search:

1. A single key word communicates multiple skills and qualifications. When a prospective employer reads the key word *sales,* they will assume you have experience in new business development, product/service presentation, negotiations, sales closings, customer relationship management, new product introduction, and more. Just one key word can have tremendous power and deliver a huge message.

2. Key words are the backbone for resume scanning technology. If a company is seeking a chief Financial Officer, they may do a key word search through hundreds of resumes to find candidates with experience in tax, treasury, cash management, currency hedging, and foreign exchange. If you don't have those words in your resume, you will be passed over.

Use your key words in all of your job search marketing communications—resumes, cover letters, interview follow-up letters, career portfolios, and more. Carefully integrate them into the text, when and where appropriate, to be sure you are communicating a complete message of "who you are" and what knowledge you bring to the organization. Note that resume scanning technology can find key words anywhere in your resume and letters, so it is not necessary to put them into a separate section.

Here are a few suggestions for how and where to incorporate your key words into your resume:

- *In the Career Summary at the beginning of your resume.* Summaries are the ideal section in which to highlight your most notable key words, and you can do this either in a paragraph format or a listing of bulleted items. By doing so, you're quickly communicating your core qualifications for immediate impact.
- *In your job descriptions.* Use key words to write powerful action statements, project highlights, achievements, and more.
- *In a separate section.* Although optional, as already noted, you may choose to summarize your key words in a separate section entitled Professional Qualifications, Skills Summary, or Areas of Expertise.

In 2002 key words are a critical component of every job seeker's resume and cover letter. You must effectively incorporate key words for your industry and profession into all of your job search communications. Without the appropriate key words, you may be at a significant loss in your search campaign and opportunities may pass you by.

—*Author's tip*

TIP #33—SELL IT TO ME; DON'T TELL IT TO ME

Read the following two sentences and see if you can tell a difference in tone and energy.

- Supervised daily production operations for a large plastics manufacturer.
- Planned, staffed, and directed daily production operations for a $2.3 million plastics manufacturer, reducing costs 14 percent and achieving profit objectives for the first time in three years.

What about a difference between these two sentences?

- Improved customer satisfaction ratings.
- Increased customer satisfaction ratings from 72 to 97 percent within three months following an intensive employee training program.

What about here?

- Reintroduced an older product line into a new customer market.
- Revitalized older product line, sold into new accounts, and generated $500,000 in new sales revenues with a 28 percent bottom-line profit.

In each of the above three samples, the first sentence "told" your reader what you did and the second sentence "sold" what you achieved. If you "sell" your success rather than "tell" your job functions, the power of your resume will increase dramatically. In turn, you will receive more interviews. Use the same strategy during your interviews and you will receive more offers. Sell your knowledge and sell your success.

—Author's tip

TIP #34—THE AGE FACTOR

If you're a candidate who is 50+ years of age, you will have to make certain decisions about your resume that only you can make. For example, do you include the fact that you graduated from college in 1964? What about your early career experience with IBM, dating from 1962 to 1970? And, what about that huge purchasing project from 1974?

Unfortunately, there are no hard and fast rules to answer these questions. You have to evaluate each individual situation, working to sell yourself and your qualifications while being sure not to date yourself out of the running.

Remember this . . . resumes are career marketing documents, *not* lifelong biographies. You do *not* have to include each and every position you've ever held. Consider summarizing the highlights of your early positions, without dates, in a paragraph at the end of your Professional Experience section. This affords you the opportunity to sell the success of those jobs without divulging the dates. It is also not mandatory that you date your college degree. Simply include the degree and the college, just not the date of graduation.

If you're tempted to include older dates because you believe that you're "supposed to," then ask yourself this question: "Why would you put something in your resume that could potentially exclude you from being considered a serious candidate?" The reality is that someone might look at your resume, see you graduated from college in 1964, and put the resume aside without ever considering your qualifications. To avoid that from happening, simply leave the dates off. When they meet you at the interview, they'll realize that you're not 39! But, you're already there and now have the opportunity to sell yourself, your expertise, and the value you bring to that organization. All of a sudden, your age becomes secondary and *not* a primary consideration for excluding you from consideration.

—*Author's tip*

TIP #35—Know Your Target: Think Like the Employer

Q: How do you catch a rabbit?

A: Hide in the garden and act like a carrot.

Q: How do you catch a squirrel?

A: Climb up a tree and act like a nut.

What have both of these hunters done? Their homework. Just as you must do in your work as a job hunter.

Each hunter above has researched and analyzed the needs of his prey, then used that information to his advantage. Research and analysis will also enable you to identify and hit your career targets. By applying these tools, you will maintain career equilibrium in this ever-changing employment environment.

As a productive member of the workforce, you have a unique and valuable set of skills and attributes. While your skills may change and grow over time, your core benefits to employers will remain somewhat constant throughout your career life. But not every skill will prove valuable to every employer. You must determine what to tell each person who reads your resume.

When you're in the market for a new job, promotion, or raise, learn to think like your quarry. As you write your resume, you must "read the mind" of the reader. What does the reader need to know about you? If you can define and quantify this on paper, you will increase your chances of proving yourself in person.

Four things will ensure your success as you write your resume.

1. *Determine the target employer's real needs.* This can be accomplished by studying posted job openings, speaking with recruiters, and calling companies for information about their openings. Needs might range from company expansion, to turnaround, to advanced technical knowledge. The employer's

goals may include an increase in brand recognition or market share, or could be as simple as reducing a manager's stress levels by adding more administrative staff.

2. *Determine your "fit" for each position.* Are you truly qualified to do the work required? Show on the resume the skills and attributes that best qualify you to achieve the target company's goals.

3. *Make it easy for the resume readers.* Explain your skill set as it applies to their needs. If, for example, you are offering your services to small employers, a broad skill set could be advantageous. If your target companies are large and segmented, your ability to do everything might appear detrimental, and you may want to emphasize a more limited, focused set of skills in line with their current requirements.

4. *Prove your worth through reproducible, quantifiable achievements that reflect your success.* Demonstrate your effectiveness by including percentages of improvement in productivity, awards for outstanding accomplishment, cost savings, profit improvements, and more. Use the achievements that most closely mirror the prospective employer's mode of operation, and detail them to include industry jargon your reader will understand. Additionally, highlight your education, training, and credentials that apply directly to the needs of the employer, or explain the link if the connection is not direct.

Make life easier for those who read your resume, and you'll make job search easier for yourself. Capture the employer's attention with proper information and appropriate wording, and you've bagged your prey. When you successfully communicate your ability to meet the employer's need, there will be a need for you. Happy hunting!

—Debra O'Reilly, CPRW, JCTC, CEIP, A First Impression
Resume Service/ ResumeWriter.com

TIP #36—TRANSLATE YOUR FEATURES INTO EMPLOYER BENEFITS

Successful execution of your job search lies in your ability to submit a position-focused resume which emphasizes the benefits you offer to each and every potential employer you are targeting. Does this mean that you have to rewrite your resume each and every time? No! What it does require is that you customize the top, "attention-grabber" section of your resume—your Career Summary, Career Profile, Summary of Qualifications, Areas of Expertise, or whatever you have chosen to call it—to the position at hand.

Here's how the process works. Once you've found a position in which you're interested, thoroughly research the company and the hiring criteria for the position. There are numerous sources you can use for your research such as Internet search engines (e.g., Google, NorthernStar), business directories (e.g., Hoovers, Thomas Register), your local public library, trade magazines, newspapers, and last but not least, your personal network of friends and relatives.

Once you have determined how your knowledge and experience relates to the company, prepare a list of your career features and the derived benefits they offer to the potential employer. Examples include:

Your Career Feature—Bachelor of Science degree in electrical engineering. *Benefit to the Employer* = a professional candidate with full capabilities and knowledge to match technical products to clients' needs.

Your Career Feature—Five years of sales experience. *Benefit to the Employer* = a candidate that will hit the ground running right after being hired and produce from day one.

Your Career Feature—Worked for competitive company. *Benefit to the Employer* = very short learning curve that will result in saving resources during the training period.

Once your list is complete, rate them from the most to the least critical for getting the employer's attention, keeping in mind the company and their specific hiring criteria. These items, particularly the benefits you offer, then form the foundation for the information that you include in your career summary. Remember, getting noticed is all about how an employer can benefit from your background, and it's your job to tell them that. Don't leave it up to the screening recruiter to interpret your features. Do it yourself and win.

—*Elie Klachkin, M.S., JCTC, Impex Services, Inc.*

TIP #37—WRITING WINNING COVER LETTERS

Cover letters are a vital component to your job search marketing toolkit. Consider this . . . 33 percent of the people you send your resume and cover letter to will never read the letter; 33 percent may read the letter if the resume interests them; the remaining 33 percent *always read the letter first*. Therefore, it goes without saying that your cover letters must be written just like your resume—as a powerful marketing communication that sells a great product—*you*.

To simplify the writing process, here's the best trick that I've ever learned. Before you start to write, ask yourself "what" you want your letter to be. Here are your two options:

1. *Do you want to focus on specific achievements and qualifications* (often the best strategy if writing in response to an advertisement)? If so, a bullet-style letter will be your best strategy. It allows you to quickly and succinctly communicate a broad range of information that should intrigue your reader and relate directly to each company's hiring qualifications.

2. *Do you want to "tell your story?"* This is often the best strategy if you're trying to sell yourself into a position for which you're not an exact fit, but would be a great candidate, or because you have a unique story to tell that will be interesting

and enticing. If this is your objective, then write your letter in paragraph style where it is easier to communicate a "story." (Obviously, that "story" should put a great deal of emphasis on your success and achievement and the value you bring to that organization.)

Once you've decided which style is right for you—bullet or paragraph—then you're ready to start writing. Begin with a powerful introductory paragraph (two to three sentences at most), then proceed with the guts of your letter as described above. You might then want to include a quick paragraph, highlighting any other relevant information or personal attributes that are important to mention. Finally, you write a short closing sentence or two that *asks for the interview*. Remember, it's the only reason that you're writing to them!

Refer to page 71 for a sample of a bullet-style cover letter; page 72 for a sample of a paragraph-style cover letter.

—Author's tip

TIP #38—USING AN INTEGRATED RESUME/COVER LETTER STRATEGY

Conducting a successful job search is greatly facilitated by using a well-written, accomplishment-oriented resume and a targeted cover letter. This cohesive package lets you clearly and dynamically articulate your credentials, qualifications, and career objective.

Key to creating a cohesive package designed to double the recipient's attention (20 seconds each per document . . . resume and letter) is linking skills noted in the Career Summary section of your resume to the needs of the hiring authority in the cover letter. Ideally, you should try to develop three specific examples of your top skills that, based on your research, align closely with the hiring authority's ex-

ANDREW R. GREENE

4889 Olson Boulevard
Casper, WY 89763

Phone: 554.345.3444
agreene@space.net

January 12, 2002

Arnold Livingston
Vice President of Technology
RIF Technologies, LLC
29 Glendale Avenue
Bethesda, MD 20816

Dear Mr. Livingston:

I am writing and forwarding my resume in anticipation that you may be interested in a candidate with more than **10 years' experience in information technology, software design and applications development**. Highlights of my career that may be of particular interest to you include:

- Pioneering innovative GPS and GIS applications.

- Evaluating organizational and operating needs to determine appropriate technologies.

- Designing, testing and implementing new software and new applications for a broad range of engineering, technical, business, administrative, analysis and reporting needs.

- Training and supervising less experienced technical and design teams.

- Developing new uses and applications for existing technologies.

- Improving performance, productivity and efficiency of operations through technological enhancement.

I am most proud of a particular IT project I managed – the development of the first land-to-air vessel tracking system for the US Marines. This was a major initiative that resulted in significant operational and security improvements for all branches of the Armed Forces.

Currently, I am confidentially exploring new professional opportunities and would welcome a personal interview at your earliest convenience. Thank you.

Sincerely,

Andrew R. Greene

Enclosure

LOUIS ARMSTRONG
212 Lucinda Drive
Monica Bay, FL 33386

Home: 331-980-3737
Office: 292-837-2837

Email: LArmstrong@aol.com
Fax: 292-837-2838

November 14, 2001

Andrea M. Miller
President
RCX Corporation
4 Main Boulevard
Albuquerque, NM 78362

Dear Ms. Miller:

Building best-in-class IT organizations is my expertise. Whether challenged to orchestrate the start-up of an new IT operation, lead an aggressive turnaround and change management, or introduce technologies to support rapid growth, I have consistently delivered strong results. My expertise lies in my ability to merge technologies with business operations to support business, financial, service, quality and performance goals. And, I have succeeded.

As the youngest Vice President and CIO in Altamonte's organization, I am personally credited with transitioning IT from a functional organization into a strategic business partner. During my tenure with the corporation, we introduced over $24 million in technology enhancements to our infrastructure, operations, systems and technical competencies. In turn, our efforts supported the company's profitable growth, market repositioning and innovative approaches to customer management.

Equally notable are my strong general management skills including, but not limited to, staffing, finance, administration, facilities and purchasing/supply management. Further, I have strong strategic planning skills and the ability to transition strategy into action and results.

Following an outstanding career with Altamonte, I ventured into the consulting arena where I have completed several interesting projects in both the US and Latin America. These experiences have clearly demonstrated my ability to effectively transcend industry, delivering appropriate IT solutions to a vast array of organizational needs.

Currently, I am exploring new executive opportunities and would welcome a personal interview at your convenience. I guarantee that the strength of my experience will add measurable value to your organization. Thank you for your consideration. If I don't hear from you within two weeks, I'll follow up with a phone call.

Sincerely,

Louis Armstrong

Enclosure

pectations. For instance, the Career Summary of a resume for a plant manager lists (among other unique descriptors and attributes) these core competencies: building lean manufacturing, streamlining operations, and maximizing profitability.

Now, how do you translate that in your cover letter? After an initial strong opening paragraph, the next paragraph should introduce and then amplify each of the three competencies from your career summary. For example, "Beyond my proven strengths in building effective organizations that consistently exceed expectations, my track record includes the following accomplishments:"

- Initiated comprehensive lean manufacturing strategy including Kaizen, Kanban, Poke Yoke, process mapping, and one-piece flow methods resulting in a 34 percent improvement in productivity for FY01 over FY00.
- Led major reorganization of production departments, implementing MAXCIM team concepts and cross-training across two shifts. Resulted in a 25 percent labor cost savings while sustaining same production levels.
- Sourced new vendors and negotiated new terms which reduced the cost of raw material procurement by better than 10 percent.

Base your selection of the competencies amplified in your cover letter on recruiter input or research into specific hiring objectives as well as the solutions you, as a candidate, can provide. Whether you are answering a classified ad or responding to an online opportunity, always take advantage of the strength of a well-crafted cover letter in developing your response (most responses to online positions allow for separate pasting of a cover letter; at a minimum, you can email an abbreviated but equally strong "selling" message as an attachment to a forwarded resume).

When creating an effective cover letter, it's important to retain your voice and your own professional sense of style. Likewise, if you've had professional assistance in developing your resume but opt to create your own cover letters, try to ensure that the look is consistent (same or similar font and point size as on your resume, matching paper for mailed responses, identical "letterhead"/contact information formatting as on your resume, etc.). Letters should never be a carbon copy of what is already presented on the resume. Spend the time necessary to understand, as closely as possible, what is being sought in the desired candidate. If you're sourcing opportunities on the Web, do some strategic research into the organizations to which you may apply. Try to integrate into your cover letter any links to breaking information that could strengthen your viability as a candidate.

For instance, after your cover letter opening to an Edward Jones' district manager (investment and financial services), you might state something along the lines of, "It was with great interest that I read in last Sunday's *New York Times* of Edward Jones' strategic campaign to build its core base of business on a community-by-community basis—deliberately sidestepping large metropolitan areas. I was struck favorably by the client-focused approach used in all of the company's marketing efforts and embrace these same values."

With competition for some of the best positions continuing to increase across most industries, anything you can do to favorably distinguish yourself from most others can really serve to elevate consideration of your overall candidacy. A "rubber-stamped" letter that's a carbon copy of what everyone else is using does little to help your efforts to secure an interview. But a creatively and uniquely written letter that is specific, linking your accomplishments to the attributes sought with very clear references, can boost your resume package to the top of the hiring manager's stack of prospects to call. You want yours in that pack, and an integrated resume/cover letter is one of the best ways to ensure that.

—*Jan Melnik, CPRW, CCM, Absolute Advantage*

TIP #39—BUILD YOUR CAREER PORTFOLIO

Career portfolios are one of the newest inventions in job search and career marketing. They are much more comprehensive than resumes and include detailed information on employment experience, accomplishments, project highlights, technical qualifications, honors and awards, publications, public speaking engagements, teaching experience, international experience, and more. Career portfolios have wide-ranging use, from the college graduate who wants to display all of his educational, work, and volunteer experience, to the senior executive who wants to provide a comprehensive summary of his entire career and all that it has entailed.

Here are some facts and figures about career portfolios:

- They tend to be many pages, from as few as 2 to 3, to as many as 10 or more. This will depend on the number of years of your experience and the specific information you choose to include.
- Each new section (e.g., professional experience, education, awards, publications) generally starts on a new page.
- Each section is comprehensive, including all related information in some degree of detail. Remember, page length is not a consideration when you're writing your portfolio.
- They are usually displayed in a rather formal presentation in some type of notebook, folder, or binder with a nicely designed cover presentation that might say something like . . . "John R. Smith, Jr.—Accounting Manager."

Although career portfolios take more time and effort to prepare than resumes, they provide you with a distinctively competitive advantage in the market. Imagine what an impression your portfolio will make (when compared to all the other candidates' resumes) at your next interview!

What's more, the process of preparing a detailed career portfolio gives you a renewed sense of self-esteem and accomplishment. By taking the time to document each and every thing you've done in your career, you'll feel good about yourself and what you have accomplished. This regenerated fervor is what will propel you through the often long and difficult job search process.

—Author's tip

TIP #40—CREATE A CAREER PORTFOLIO CD

The overall idea of portfolios is not new. Artists and academics have used this medium in their job search for decades. What is new, however, is that a present-day portfolio must continually change to reflect the individual's career within a fast-moving economy. The ability to adapt one's documents to match newly acquired skills is of utmost importance when approaching employers. New advancements within the computer technology world and this notion of adaptability have enabled portfolio usage to make the transition into mainstream job search. Subsequently, a portfolio CD has become a modern job searcher's ally allowing for the flexibility, adaptability, and portability that is necessary in today's world.

The multimedia presentations on these CDs can be accomplished by even the weakest of computer novices. Therefore anyone, whatever field of employment they are pursuing, can benefit from this marketing tool. Having said this, how exactly does one begin? Do you need programming experience? What software is available to help? What information do you put into a portfolio CD to make it an effective aid in landing an interview and a new job? Although your portfolio, by the pure essence of its definition will be unique, there are some guidelines that can be used to help create a multimedia presentation that will separate you from the rest.

1. Formulate your information into categories before starting to build your presentation. This step will save you time and energy in the long run. Using headers to organize your material

will help you not only in the creation aspect but in the addition of "hyperlinks" (shortcuts to facilitate navigation through your portfolio). Some examples of categories you might want to add include Professional Goals, Employment Experience, Formal Education/Training, On-the-Job Training, Technology Skills, Public Speaking, and Publications.

2. The use of a CD burner and scanner are imperative to the transformation. These two tools are a must if you are to move your linear portfolio into the 3-D world. Having said this, there is no need to rush out and purchase expensive equipment to put together your portfolio. You can actually gain access to these from various computer cafés or chain stores such as Kinko's where, for a minimal fee, you can scan or burn your items to create your portfolio CD.

   The step-by-step procedures on the software incorporated into the operating systems of these two tools are simple to use and require no further explanation. You should, however, remember a few points:

   - Save your scanned item using as little memory space as possible. You do not want your document to be so large that it cannot be viewed from an ordinary PC.

   - Ensure that the CD burner you are using is compatible for viewing both PC and Mac systems.

   - Use your imagination and just "scan and burn" to your heart's content.

3. Use HTML (Hypertext Mark-Up Language) as the method of encoding the way your portfolio will look on your CD-ROM. Using HTML has become increasingly easier with the introduction of Web page authoring tools such as Dreamweaver by Macromedia, FrontPage Express found on Microsoft's Internet Explorer, and Composer from Netscape's Communicator browser. These programs will allow your portfolio to be viewed through an HTML browser that almost all PCs have. This format will also allow for the smooth transformation of

your portfolio CD into an electronic version, thereby allowing emailing or Web posting.

If you would rather run a stand-alone application, meaning one that does not require the viewer to have any additional software, the best way would be to use Macromedia Flash. The alternative to HTML would be to either use MS Word, which does not allow video and animation additions, or to use PowerPoint which requires the viewer to have this software. Although viable, both of these options do not compare with HTML in terms of depth in application and usability.

4. Use rewritable CD-ROMs to be able to update your portfolio at a moment's notice. The whole strategy behind the use of a portfolio CD is its flexibility in allowing for change as new skills are gained. The more expensive CD-ROM-Rs (rewritable) will allow you to amend your portfolio, thereby maintaining this idea of adaptability. Other CD-ROMs only allow you to burn something to it once, defeating your ability to manipulate the presentation over time. The major advice in this realm: Pay the extra initially and it will amount to huge savings in the long run.

5. Get help from an expert! If you are a person who is intimidated by anything technical, no problem! Approach a professional resume writer or career coach to help you assemble and produce your portfolio CD. These professionals are trained to assemble a package that will help you win your dream job!

At a recent international job fair, it was the norm, not the exception, for applicants to deliver a portfolio CD to prospective employers. Written to represent individuality, one can see how these portfolios give job seekers an edge that the traditional 2-D resume does not. The use of a portfolio CD can ultimately help you land the job of your dreams by marketing the world's best product—*you!*

—*Nicole Miller, BA, RRP, CPRW, IJCTC, Mil-Roy Consultants*

TIP #41—Resumes and Money Don't Mix

How often have you responded to an advertisement that asked for your salary history (what you've made in the past) or your salary requirements (current salary expectations)? Your answer is, most likely, quite often. Always remember that your resume is *not* the appropriate platform for discussing your salary or compensation plan. Rather, include that information in your cover letter where you can easily modify it as appropriate for each individual position, each company, and each recruiter. And, in fact, statistics from numerous studies show that even if you don't provide that information as requested, if the company is interested in you, they'll call anyway.

—Author's tip

TIP #42—Be Honest and Credible

Selling your achievements, success, and qualifications is what writing career marketing documents (e.g., resumes, cover letters, career portfolios, follow-up letters) is all about. Your challenge is to demonstrate, on paper, that you are well qualified, offer unique skills and talents, and will bring measurable value to the hiring company.

However, you must be 100 percent honest and credible in each and every thing you write. Work hard to "paint the picture you want someone to see"—who you are and what you offer—but be honest and only push as hard as is realistic. If you ever have to defend something you've written in your resume or cover letter, you will have lost. There is rarely, if ever, any way to reclaim your credibility.

—Author's tip

CHAPTER 4

Success Strategies for Job Search and Career Marketing

TIP #43—JOB SEARCH IS A JOB!

The more time and energy you devote to your job search, the more resumes you get out, the more aggressively you network, the more recruiters you contact, the faster your search will proceed. If employed, commit 20 hours per week exclusively to your search campaign. If not currently employed, commit a minimum of 40 hours a week. If you sit passively and wait for opportunities to find you, you will be waiting a very long time.

If you think dedicating 20 to 40 hours a week on your job search sounds like a lot . . . then you're right! But job search success depends on your level of commitment, including planning, taking risks, and following up on leads you produce. First, decide whether you are capable of carrying out a successful, self-directed job search. If you feel you might need some guidance, knowledge, or accountability essential to moving onto greener pastures, then seek guidance from a career industry professional immediately.

Remember, the best investment in your job search is hard work through

Learning all you can: Regardless of your circumstances, get out there and read *everything* you can. Knowledge is power!

Determining your job objective: It's always easier to look for a specific job rather than pursuing a variety of career objectives.

Identifying your skills: In order to stay ahead of your competition, know yourself and what job skills you offer an employer that are better than the abilities of others who are competing in your job market.

Researching the job market: Research hiring practices and companies within your field of interest, and discover what criteria and demands are most important. Every little bit you know can help you get your foot in the door!

Marketing yourself right: Not only will having the right job search tools build your confidence, it will help you to stand out from the competition. Dynamic cover letters, targeted resumes, and timely follow-up communiqués are a *must*!

Knowing what employers want: Learn what employers are seeking and how they look for it. Be prepared for your interviews with this knowledge and communicate your confidence.

Developing job leads: Get in the game through referrals and leads. Follow up on leads and network, network, and network!

Using time wisely: Establish a daily action plan and keep an organized job search campaign crucial to reaching your goal.

Since a job search campaign does involve a huge time commitment, a systematic approach is necessary for that successful quest. An applied work plan with predictable results will dramatically minimize the amount of anxiety that many people experience during a job transition.

—*Denise Lupardo, Denise's Office Support & Resumes*

TIP #44—MARKET YOURSELF BROADLY

There are dozens of ways to land interview opportunities with target employers. . . . You will learn about many of them in this book. But here's a surprise: Although it is widely believed that networking is the most effective method of search, a Census Bureau survey of 10 million job seekers tells us that, in fact, applying directly to employers is the top-ranked method used to land new positions. (Networking was second and answering classified advertisements third.) Making quality contacts with target employers over the telephone and submitting a well-constructed cover letter and resume will locate opportunities early, thereby reducing or even eliminating your competition completely!

How to Begin: Develop Clear Goals

To be productive, you must be organized and set clear and attainable goals. Select your company targets by deciding what is important to you for a long-term commitment. For example, in which industry are you most interested? What size of an organization do you prefer? Is location important? Corporate culture? Amount of travel? Salary? Do you need additional education or training to attain your career goal? What else is important to you? Now's the time to decide, so consider all the relevant issues early and you won't waste valuable time.

Make a List

Make a list of employers—local, national and/or international—that will be interested in hiring someone with your education and experience. Good sources for this information are your local library and Internet directories such as:

Poor's Register of Corporations, Directors and Executives
Dun & Bradstreet's Directories

Moody's Directories

Various Association Listings

Include the company's name, address, and phone number, plus the names and titles of those professionals and managers who might have the authority to hire you. *Note:* There is usually only a 50–80 percent accuracy rate for this data, so you must verify the information before proceeding.

Tip: If you are speaking with an operator to verify your contact information, be polite, but you must sound authoritative and businesslike, giving the impression that you have every reason in the world to be provided with the information you're asking about. If, for example, you have a list of four vice presidents and you need to know which one is in charge of marketing, approach the operator this way, selecting one of the four names at random: "I need to check my information. Mr. X is still the vice president of marketing, correct?" If the answer is no, then say, "Oh, I must have my names confused. Who is the current vice president of marketing?"

If you do not have a list of choices, try this approach: "I'm updating our records for my company. Would you be so kind as to give me some assistance? Who is the current vice president of marketing?"

You should begin with a list of about 25 companies and contact names. One of these companies may be more likely to hire you than another, so prioritize your list and begin at the top. It's helpful to keep the list on your PC, so you can easily make changes. Keep close track of the dates and results of your contacts, and make sure to follow up.

Practice, Practice, Practice!

Practice giving a 30-second ad about what you do and what value you have to offer. Rehearse your script with others to develop a smooth presentation. Before long you'll be able to deliver the message effectively and confidently and will be amazed at your results!

Tip: When you're making business phone calls, dress for business. Doing so will significantly improve your delivery . . . no kidding!

Tip: When you're making calls, stand up. It will give your voice an air of power and authority. Really, it works . . . try it!

Tip: When you're talking, smile! It actually changes the tone of your voice. The "smiling voice" can get through many doors that are otherwise closed.

Cast a Broad Net

To further increase the likelihood of your success, don't restrict your-self to a single strategy. Remember to continue networking, look for and respond to classified and/or trade journal ads, and keep an eye on industry-specific Internet sites. The more you do, the better. After all, landing your dream job is much like fishing . . . the more hooks you have in the water, the better your chances of getting a bite!

—*Debbie Ellis, CPRW, Phoenix Career Group*

TIP #45—A LESSON IN SALES 101

One way to approach a job search is to view it like a sales campaign for a unique, but highly desirable product—*you.*

As every good sales professional knows, the sales process involves several well-defined steps. These include prospecting, qualifying leads, cold calling, assessing customer needs, making sales presentations, conducting follow-up, and closing the sale. Each of these activities has a corollary in the job search process.

Prospecting/Qualifying Leads

Explore the vital steps in acquiring and working leads. In your case, leads are generated by networking, searching newspaper ads, surfing the Web, or posting your resume on job search websites. Once you start identifying prospects, you need to qualify these leads. For each potential employer under consideration, try to answer these questions:

- Does this company have current openings for someone with your skills?
- Even if there aren't advertised openings, is this a company that is likely to have a need for someone like you?
- Is this truly a company for which you want to work? Even though you need a job and want to get back to work, there are employers that you may wish to avoid.
- Can you identify the key decision makers in the firm? For a job applicant, this would be the hiring manager or the lead person in the department in which you want to work. Although human resource people are part of the process, they often are not the ones actually making the hiring decision. An astute sales professional doesn't waste time talking to people who can't make a buying decision.
- Do you know anyone currently working for the company? Commonly known as networking, you need to make friends, relatives, coworkers, and so on, aware of your job search. You don't want to bluntly ask them to help you get a job, but if you make them aware that you're looking and share a copy of your resume with them, they may be more than happy to steer you in the direction of someone who can hire you.

Cold Calling

In addition to applying for advertised openings, an important part of a successful job search is approaching companies that haven't advertised, but nonetheless may need someone with your skills. By following the steps mentioned above, especially networking, you can identify companies worth targeting, even if they aren't actively seeking employees.

A top sales rep really earns her money by finding the customer that didn't even know he needed her product/service. If you can get your resume in the hands of the right person within a company, he may decide to take advantage of an opportunity to bring in a new person. They may have a need, but have avoided going through the search process for any of a number of reasons.

Assessing Customer Needs

Just like a sales professional, you need to research the prospect (employer) and ask questions in the interview to assess their needs. Many hiring authorities say that the questions an applicant asks are as important as the answers given to employer questions. Visit the company's website, or go to the library, and find out as much as possible about the company, its products, and its current business challenges.

In the interview, ask thoughtful questions about the company that will help you understand their needs and how you can fulfill those needs.

Making Sales Presentations

Once you understand the company's needs, use the interview to communicate how you (the product) can be a solution to their business problem. This may sound a little daunting, but remember that you're selling a product that you know and believe in—yourself.

Typically, at some point, the interviewer will give you the opportunity to talk about yourself. This may be at the beginning of the interview, at the end, or both. Rehearse your 90-second commercial that you can deliver at the beginning of the interview if asked "Tell me about yourself." Every sales pro worth his salt has a brief synopsis of his company and product always ready to deliver in any setting— social gathering, cocktail lounge after work, or business meeting. You need to develop the same type of brief description of your career and your current goals.

Once you've had the chance to ask questions and gain a better understanding of what the employer is seeking, you can end your interview with examples of how your experience, education, and skill sets coincide with their needs and can help them address their business challenges.

Conducting Follow-Up

After the presentation, remember to follow up. Send a thank-you letter immediately after the interview to everyone who participated. This letter should reiterate why you're the person for the job and mention any points that weren't discussed in the interview that may strengthen your candidacy.

Understand the decision-making timeline and follow up with phone calls so that the employer remembers you and recognizes your enthusiastic interest in working for them.

Closing the Sale

If you get called back for a second or third interview, you've obviously made a good impression. During these subsequent interviews, try to zero in on the ways you can fit into the employer's corporate culture and be a productive contributor to their success.

Try to let the interviewer(s) mention salary first and be careful to consider the entire compensation package when making a decision. If they ask you what salary you are looking for, the correct response is, "Are you making me an offer?" At that point, let the negotiating begin. Carefully read Chapter 7 for expert advice on negotiating your salary and compensation package.

The good news is that you only need a single sale to meet your quota. If you assess the market, contact qualified potential leads, make a presentation showing how you fit their needs, and follow up to close the sale, you and your new employer will have that win-win scenario every good sales executive hopes to achieve.

—Arnold G. Boldt, CPRW, JCTC, Arnold-Smith Associates

TIP #46—Create Your Own Personal Brand

Job search in the twenty-first century means transitioning your thinking from traditional job search methodology (presenting yourself as the sum of your job titles) to embracing leading-edge personal marketing strategies (selling yourself as the sum of your intellectual capital).

Job search in the twenty-first century is not about resumes, want ads, the Internet, and recruiters. It is about career building. It is about presenting yourself as a product. It is about marketing yourself as a package of features and benefits. It is about understanding that an employer will interview and hire you not for your titles and job history, but for your skills and accomplishments.

Career building in the twenty-first century requires that you create an ever-evolving personal brand and position yourself in the marketplace as a solutions provider with a compelling value proposition.

Accomplishments are the building blocks of personal branding. They are the quantifiable results of your skills and attributes. They are the predictors of future successes—the results that say "I did this for XYZ Company and I can do something even better for you." Once you have identified these prime predictors, use savvy networking to get the message of your brand into the marketplace, and constantly increase your industry knowledge to keep yourself at the leading edge of your peer group.

In good economic times or bad, employers have as much anxiety about hiring the right person for the job as you have in finding the right job. Much rides on their correct decision and anything that helps them to make an informed choice is welcome. That is where personal branding comes in.

Think about this: If you had a sick child and your doctor recommended a certain brand of medication, you would use that brand. If you were hosting an important event and wanted the best refreshments available, you would purchase name-brand products. If you wanted to buy a new appliance, you would likely purchase a major brand after researching reputations and service records.

Brands have reputations built on quality and benefit to the consumer. They have performed well in the past and are expected to do so in the future. There is a trust factor involved in purchasing a branded "known quantity."

Here's the parallel to job search and career building: You craft your brand just like any good commercial enterprise does. You provide quality, you prove your benefit, and you market both. You do it over and over again until you have achieved a market presence. You then continue your efforts to dominate your market.

You provide quality by doing your job in ways that contribute solutions and value to your company. You are never satisfied with an average outcome. You always strive to exceed expectations. You motivate your peers and your staff to achieve their best. You are a leader, a resource, and a driving force.

You prove your benefit by making money for your company, or by creating efficiency for your company, or by building innovative processes for your company, or by generating customer loyalty for your company, or by achieving any number of bottom-line results. And you do so repeatedly.

You market your quality and your benefit by raising the awareness of your brand in your target market—that of your industry, field, or discipline. Build your personal and industry networks. Let your boss know what you have done; do not assume she knows—she is just as busy as you are. Build alliances within your peer group and your management team—not through politics but through solid performance; if you help them do a project better or faster they will remember you and your expertise. Become known as an expert in your industry—join professional associations, speak at conferences, and be interviewed or quoted by the media. The more you become known as a solid yet innovative professional, the higher the trust factor, the better the brand.

The outcome? When your name is mentioned, someone will say, "Oh, I know John, he gave me a hand on the Cisco project. He really knows his stuff." If someone is looking for a candidate for a position and asks around their network, they will hear about John who was "Great with the Cisco project! And I heard him speak at our convention last year. He really knows his stuff." If a recruiter is looking for a few solid candidates and asks her circle of contacts for some leads she may hear, "I think you should speak to John. He's totally up to speed with that new technology. He led his team to bring in the Cisco project under budget, three months early and with no bugs after the implementation. The company got a bonus for the great job and got the follow-on contract, too. John was interviewed by CNN's business reporter after that one."

Notice something lacking here? No job titles are mentioned.... John is known by his actions, not his titles. And that's the last important component of brand building. Job titles are secondary to knowledge and performance. Titles can change from company to company. Skills and accomplishments are abilities and actions tied to solutions and revenue, not prestige or corporate hierarchy. Skills and accomplishments get you interviewed and hired. Titles may get you an interview, but titles without strong action will certainly not get you a job or build your brand.

Personal branding will allow you to demonstrate to employers that you are the person who can help them quickly surpass their goals, create innovation, manage change, or respond to whatever need they have. Personal branding will allow employers to learn about you from other sources and have a trust factor going into the interview. In an employees' market (many jobs), you will garner the best salary, perks, and flexibility in the job of your choice. In an employers' market (fewer jobs), you will beat the competition, securing the best position and compensation available.

If you do not prepare to market yourself as a consummate problem solver and out-of-the-box thinker, you will have no ability to react with lightning speed to our changing marketplace. It is the well-prepared, yet nimble professionals who will stay branded, stay competitive, and land on their feet no matter what the environment.

—*Deborah Wile Dib, CCM, NCRW, CPRW, CEIP, JCTC,*
Advantage Resumes of New York

TIP #47—FINDING AND LEVERAGING SPOT OPPORTUNITIES

You will be more likely to find a new position by reading the business and local news pages of your newspaper than screening the classified ads. What you should be looking for are "spot opportunities."

A spot opportunity is reported information which can be used by a job seeker to uncover or create employment opportunities. Anything that has happened, is happening, or might happen in any working environment of interest can present a spot opportunity. The following examples illustrate a few of the dozens of different types of spot opportunities:

- News of an executive's promotion or the recruitment of a new senior manager is a basic indication of opportunity. Rarely will an executive keep all of an inherited staff. Several new hires usually occur during the first six months.

- Raising new capital through public offerings or major bank financing normally indicates that a firm is planning business development or trying to solve a financial crunch. In most instances, some portion of the new funds will be spent on hiring additional personnel.

- New buildings or new office space leases typically suggest business expansion. Usually a firm will move rapidly to fill up expensive space by hiring from outside.

- A new fiscal year (usually a new calendar year) is an excellent time to look for spot opportunities. Companies have a new budget and can structure themselves to accomplish newly defined goals.

The techniques for capitalizing on spot opportunities are among the most powerful approaches of all interview-producing methods. It takes a modest amount of work to locate these spot opportunities and a little creative effort to capitalize on them. However, your investment of time is likely to produce exceptional rewards.

Philosophically, all change represents an opportunity, and change is inevitable. Companies need help to cope with change, and you can provide that help. Spot opportunities can be advantageous to a job seeker in the following ways:

- They allow an applicant to have control over "being in the right place at the right time."

- Capitalizing on a spot opportunity can give you a competitive edge over candidates who appear to be qualified. Jobs are awarded to individuals for reasons other than the face value of their qualifications. Showing originality, initiative, foresight, and more, will positively influence a hiring decision.

- A spot opportunity approach suggests to the reader that you possess desirable qualities such as being creative, unique, perceptive, and resourceful. You demonstrate a desirable aggressive nature and make a dramatic, positive impression.

- Your spot opportunity appeal focuses on an immediate need of the organization at an opportune time.

- Making yourself known through a meaningful communication saves an organization money on recruiting expenses. They will prefer you, in part, for this reason.

- By using spot opportunities, you increase your marketability by avoiding competition. The concept allows you to attract attention and create interviews before competition emerges.

- Since a specific position is not necessarily defined, the employer is more open to suggestions and general discussion. The opportunity to create an ideal job description is more possible.

- Barriers normally erected by the human resources department and secretaries can be circumvented by using spot opportunities. For the most part, you are communicating directly with the hiring decision maker.

- The spot opportunity allows you to make a tailored letter response, which highlights relevant information about the company's situation and your capabilities. This approach does not require you to furnish complete details concerning your background. Liabilities can be successfully suppressed.

- Your correspondence can serve as an ego boost to the reader and be quite favorably received. It shows that the public is aware of the company's activities. Your contact can be a pleasant interruption in a hectic business day. You will be fostering a friendship at a high level and working to develop what could become a valuable personal contact.

- The very approach you are using indicates you are an involved and resourceful individual with a sincere interest in the organization. Firms like to hire people who really want to work for them.

Where to Find Spot Opportunities

You don't have to look far for spot opportunities. They are passing in front of you on a daily basis. Up to this point, you have probably not capitalized upon this information. You'll find them in:

Newspapers. Well-known newspapers such as *The Wall Street Journal* and newspapers from your area of geographical preference (*Miami Business Journal, Atlanta Business Chronicle, Houston Business Journal*, etc.) provide a wealth of information in feature articles, product or company advertisements, highlights of personalities in business, industry surveys, and the classified sections.

Magazines. General news and business magazines such as *Fortune, Business Week, Forbes, Venture, U.S. News & World Report, Time, Newsweek*, and periodicals from a specific geographical area (*Business Atlanta, New Jersey Monthly, New England Business*, etc.) can provide an abundant source of spot opportunity situations.

Trade Journals. Industry and professional magazines are an excellent way to keep abreast of the current happenings in a particular field of interest to you. *Business Rates and Publication Data* is a business library resource book that can give you complete information concerning types of trade journals. Frequently, specialists and individuals who have been in their field for many years are surprised when they see a complete list of pertinent trade publications. Often there will be several sources that are unfamiliar, yet very valuable to a job seeker.

Professional Journals. Many associations publish professional magazines, directories, trade catalogs, or newsletters. Valuable data concerning professional trends and names of key individuals can be obtained from a journal article or membership directory. Often, trade and professional associations will have formal or informal position referral services. They serve a clearinghouse role, matching candidates to known job or position openings. Information regarding associations can be obtained in the *Encyclopedia of Associations*.

Television and Radio. The news, commercials, commentaries, and talk shows may also provide information on new products, businesses, consumer issues, and opportunities.

Being There! Don't overlook the power that first-hand information can offer you. Attendance at speeches, seminars, trade shows, and conventions are naturally part of any professional's career development. You do not have to be an organization member to attend most events; a business card is often sufficient for admission.

Use this time to obtain pertinent information regarding products, industries, and/or key individuals. This information can be in the form of a trade show directory, product literature, and so on. Chance meetings, social events, or an impromptu walk-in to a company of interest are also ways in which you can gather information and generate interviews.

Now that you know what spot opportunities are, go find yours.

—*Don Skipper, MS, MMAS, CCM, R. L. Stevens*
& Associates, Inc.

TIP #48—Use Recruiters to Your Advantage

There are many strategies that job seekers can deploy to find their next career position and one of the most productive can be working with professional recruiters. If you want to remain local, the best place to start is with your telephone book, under the categories of recruiter, employment agency, and staffing agency. If your search is more broad-based, then go to the Web for the numerous recruiter resources you'll find online.

Recruiters fall into one of two categories: contingency and retained. Both of these refer to the type of relationship that the recruiter has with the client company for which they are working, for it is the company who pays the recruitment fees, *not* the individual job seeker. Let's explore the similarities and differences between the two in more detail.

In a contingency arrangement, the recruiter or employment agency does not get paid unless, and until, the client company actually hires the applicant referred. The recruiter or agency is most likely working for, or at least has contact with, a large number of client companies. The fee paid is usually on a sliding scale based on the first-year starting salary of the applicant and is capped at a certain level (usually 30 percent). That means if the applicant's starting salary were $60,000, the top fee would be $18,000.

Most recruiters do offer some form of a guarantee so that if the applicant quits before a predetermined time, usually 90 days, the recruiter has the opportunity to find a new applicant or to refund a prorated portion of the fee. The primary things to remember about contingency recruiters are that they get paid only if they fill a job, and payment is based on your starting salary.

In a retained arrangement, a client company hires a recruiter to fill all of the positions for their company during a defined period of time, usually six months to one year. The two parties agree on an amount for services and that amount is paid over the term of the contract. It doesn't matter how many positions are filled or what the starting salaries are; the fee remains the same. This is very similar to an attorney that works for a company on "retainer." The primary things to remember about retained recruiters is that they are paid whether you get the job or not, and your starting salary has no impact on their compensation.

Does all of this mean that one type of recruiter will work harder for you than another? Could it mean that a contingency recruiter might have a stronger sense of urgency to make a placement than a retained search recruiter? Not necessarily. By and large the majority of recruiters are professional people who will work hard for you either way. In fact, many recruiters have both retained and contingency accounts.

Here are a few other essential facts you need to know about working with recruiters:

- As stated earlier, client companies pay recruiter fees, both contingent and retained. As such, smart recruiters who value their time will have some type of screening process to weed out candidates who are not serious "players." The last thing any recruiter wants is to waste time putting a candidate "in play" only to find out that they weren't really interested.

- Work with as many recruiters as you can. These are *not* exclusive relationships.

- Most recruiters will ask you to sign a contract. As with any other contract, read it carefully before signing. It should not bind you to any "hidden" fees or exclusivity to that recruiter.

- Contact recruiters who specialize in your industry and/or profession. Generally, they will have more contacts for you because of their specializations and, in turn, may provide better results.

- "Lay it on the line" with recruiters. Be honest in communicating your salary expectations, discuss any special health care or educational needs your family may have, and alert the recruiter to any other items that would impact your decision to take a job. They need to know this information to make the "right match."

Most importantly, always remember that recruiters get paid to find the "best" candidates there are, so always be at your best when working with them. Your next job depends on it!

—*Norm Gavlick, Gavlick Personnel Services, Inc.*

TIP #49—The Hiring Authorities May Not Be Where You Think They Are

Most people in career transition don't want to relocate for their next job. They want to stay right where they are. Perhaps they own a home. Their families and friends are close by. Their children are involved in their schools and activities. And, the family has ties to the community. The prospect of moving and putting down roots again is not one they want to face.

If you're one of these people, you'll want to start your job search in your own community. However, the hiring authority (the person you need to talk to) is often in a different location. How do you find them?

Finding Employers

Lots of local businesses are controlled by people from out of town. Take a look at the businesses in your community. Small retailers are generally locally owned and operated. But take a stroll through the mall, any shopping mall of consequence, and see if you know the location of headquarters for each store. Chances are, you won't.

This is not only true of retailers, but many other businesses. For example, where I live, *all* the major supermarket chains, department stores, and banks are based elsewhere. While these companies may hire locally for some jobs, much hiring takes place elsewhere—at corporate headquarters. Use print and online resources to research company information that you need to find the hiring managers.

Finding Recruiters

Many employers use recruiters (sometimes called "headhunters") to help them fill positions. Recruiters scour the entire nation for the right candidates for the assignment at hand. The employers pay the recruiter a sizable fee for their services. The well-advised job seeker needs to find the recruiters who specialize in the job seeker's field or they will never know about the job opportunities that might be local. Recruiters rarely advertise the assignments they are working on.

Some recruiters develop specialized knowledge and contacts over time and these recruiting firms are engaged by companies all over the country because of their expertise. Recruiting firms might have contacts in a particular industry (e.g., health care, technology, hospitality, aviation), while others may focus on particular types of jobs (e.g., sales, accounting, computer programming, chemical engineering). To optimize your response, find the recruiters who specialize in your profession in your industry. Those are the recruiters who want to know about you and will most likely have the right opportunities for you. You can find these recruiters in books at your local library or through a number of online services.

In years past, when long distance telephone service was relatively expensive, recruiting tended to be local. Today, low-cost, long-distance telephone service has made it possible for recruiters to work the entire nation. A telephone and 5¢ per-minute long-distance cost is all a first-class recruiting firm needs to make the world a very small place. As such, you are not limited to using recruiters just in your area. It is quite possible a recruiter in Chicago is looking for a candidate for a position in Ft. Myers, Florida.

Finding Venture Capital Firms

Venture capital firms often provide the "seed" money for start-up businesses. Over time, they may accumulate interests in many successful businesses all over the country and around the globe. Consequently, hiring does not necessarily take place at the local level. The wise job seeker needs to find the headquarters of the venture capital firm in order to get an interview. The owners, the VC firm, may be next door to the company or thousands of miles away.

On an individual business basis, ownership is often easy to determine. Walk in and ask. Other than that, refer to print and online resources to research information and find venture capital firms that invest in your industry. Be aware that contacting venture capital firms is *not* an appropriate search strategy for every job seeker. These types of campaigns are generally most appropriate for individuals looking for senior management and executive positions. Typically, the VC firms themselves hire the leaders of each of the companies that they own and the rest of the hiring is done at the company level.

The lesson to be learned here is that you need to expand your geography during your job search to an area much larger than just the region in which you wish to work. You'd be amazed to know that hiring for the company 10 miles from your home is handled in an office 2000 miles away!

—Bob Bronstein, Pro/File Research

TIP #50—CONSIDER A SPONSOR LETTER CAMPAIGN

Sponsor letters are a relatively new phenomena in today's job search market and can give you a tremendously competitive advantage if you have the right sponsor. With these campaigns, your sponsor is introducing you to companies rather than you having to make the contact. Here's how it works:

> *Step 1.* Identify a potential sponsor, an individual you know well and who has high-level personal contacts in companies that would be interested in someone with your experience.

Step 2. Ask your sponsor to write and send a letter of introduction on your behalf to 10 to 20 of his personal contacts. What you want is a letter that communicates that you are a great candidate and a great hire, and the company should see you immediately. Obviously, the language of the letter will not be that aggressive, but that's the concept you want the letter to get across. You can even tell your sponsor that you'd be happy to draft the letter if that would be easier.

Step 3. Get the name, address, email, and phone number of all of your sponsor's contacts and use that information to follow up five to seven days later. By phone is the best method; email if you must. Hopefully, you will have heard from several of the companies by then and already have scheduled interviews, so follow-up may not be required.

Sponsor campaigns can yield tremendous results. Suppose you've worked in the purchasing department of Lucent Technologies for years. Now, you're relocating and need to find a new position. If you can get your director to contact his/her colleagues on your behalf, you're halfway to a great new opportunity.

—Author's tip

TIP #51—BYPASS THE HUMAN RESOURCES DEPARTMENT

Whenever possible, you want to interview with a hiring manager and *not* the Human Resources Department. HR professionals have vital jobs at their companies, but are generally not hiring managers and decision makers (unless it's for a position in HR). Often their job is to screen resumes based on a specific set of criteria that has been outlined by the hiring manager. They receive a resume, match it to the hiring qualifications and, if it matches, forward it to the hiring manager. There is no room in the process for individual interpretation; it's simply a matching process.

However, this is *not* what you want to happen. Your objective is to get your resume in front of the appropriate decision maker (e.g., President, VP of Sales, VP of Manufacturing, Distribution Manager, Customer Service Director). These individuals have the power to make a hiring decision and get you through the HR process. Therefore, when contacting companies to explore hiring opportunities, always address your calls and correspondence to the decision maker.

In situations where you are responding to an advertisement that directs you to forward your resume to the HR Department, do as instructed. But, don't stop there. Find the name of the hiring manager and send your resume and cover letter to that individual as well. This "double-hit" method can be extremely effective. I have witnessed a number of instances when a job seeker received a "Thanks, but no thanks" letter from the HR Department just as they were getting a call from the hiring manager at that same company to schedule an interview!

—Author's tip

TIP #52—IMAGE IS EVERYTHING!

The job search process is a series of separate steps, but they are all interrelated and all have the same goal—positioning you as the perfect candidate. Does your paper image reflect your professional image, and vice versa?

Start with a letter of introduction that speaks to a reader's need and entices him to learn more about you. Create a resume that is a marketing tool (different from an employment application) that speaks to the unique value you bring to an organization and conveys a visual image of your ability, confidence, and professionalism.

Any email communication you send in response to an inquiry from a prospective employer should reinforce that professional image. Apply the same standards of a traditional, conservative snail mail response to every email communication.

Prior to an interview, call the receptionist or the interviewer's secretary to get specific directions. Take a few minutes to speak personally with her when you arrive for your interview. Treat this person like your new best friend. When someone goes out of their way to be kind and courteous to you, do you remember that moment and comment to everyone you talk to about how kind that person was? Friendly, courteous behavior is not quickly forgotten. Don't miss out on the opportunity to convey your professionalism and character to everyone you meet.

When you walk in the room for your interview, that first visual impression should match the one the employer has created in his mind. Your dress, eye contact, handshake, ice-breaking comments, vocabulary, body language, and thoughtful questions should perpetuate that image. Convey enthusiasm and a strong outward focus that communicates you are there to help the company achieve its goals, solve its challenges, and add value to the bottom line.

Use solid C-A-R (challenge, action, result) examples to show the value you bring to an organization. Think about the last time you attended a speech. What was it that you most remembered from that 15- or 20-minute presentation? Was it the facts and statistics, or was it when the speaker actually summed up what he said with a personal testimonial that caught and held your interest? Don't just tell *what* you did, tell *how* you did it.

Finally, take advantage of a thank-you letter to confirm your interest, reiterate your most vital qualifications, convey your good manners, and solidify your image as a valuable asset. Send it out within 24 hours of your interview. You can strengthen your position as a qualified candidate by simply being courteous.

From that first piece of paper that positions you above your competition to the last thank-you note you write, create a professional marketing campaign that conveys a positive image consistent with the position you are seeking and you will win.

—*Cynthia L. Kraft, CPRW, JCTC, CCM, Executive Essentials*

TIP #53—CREATE AN INTEGRATED CAREER MARKETING PLAN

Here's a typical conversation between a job seeker and a resume writer:

> Employment Seeker [with a long face]: "This resume isn't working. I need a resume rewrite."
>
> Resume Writer/Career Coach: "I see. And how many resumes have you distributed? How many contacts have you made?"
>
> Employment Seeker: "Oh, about five or six per week, answering ads on the Web and in the newspaper."
>
> Resume Writer/Career Coach: "And what other resources are you using for job leads?"
>
> Employment Seeker [with a blank look]: "Other resources?"

It is the employment seeker that is not working here, not the resume!

Job search is marketing. You have a product to sell and you must sell it as you would any other product—by using *all* the appropriate marketing and distribution channels. You can use the following strategy to achieve success.

Work to a Plan

A very successful client recently commented to me that he attributed his work and life success to his outstanding planning and project management ability. For every challenge he faces, personal or business, he analyzes the situation, develops a project plan, and works the plan.

For a successful career transition, you want to do the same. Plan your daily activities, making sure that you devote a specified amount of time each and every day to the project. Keep careful records of your contacts and a calendar for follow-ups, networking meetings, and other events. Diligently work your project plan.

Tap a Variety of Resources

Integral to the success of your plan will be the employment search resources that you use. Not all resources are appropriate in every instance, but you will definitely want to ensure that your search campaign is multi- rather than one-dimensional.

Networking will, most likely, be your #1 employment search resource. Depending on what survey you reference, somewhere between 70 percent and 80 percent of all hires are made through networking of some sort. That leaves 20 percent to 30 percent for *all* other resources combined. And, although recruiters can certainly be a good resource, they actually account for only about 10 percent of all hires. So, if you have not aggressively tapped your network, you are not playing the odds to your advantage.

Many people believe that they do not have a network. This could not be further from the truth, unless they were raised in the wild by a pack of wolves and have never contacted another human being! Read Chapter 5 of this book for great networking tips.

While continuously cultivating and growing your network is item #1 in your employment search project plan, you are by no means finished. You also need to access resources that account for the other 20 to 30 percent of successful job leads. These include:

Print Advertisements. Regularly scan newspapers, business journals, and trade/industry publications for (1) companies recruiting for your target position, (2) companies advertising for other positions that may have an unadvertised opening, and (3) companies that are highlighted as growing/changing and may need someone just like you to help them through the challenges they face.

Online (Web or Email) Distribution. This is a quick, low-cost way to gain incredibly broad exposure of your credentials to potential employers, recruiters, and venture capitalists, both nationally and worldwide. Primary methods include posting your resume on job boards and in resume databases, and using one of the many excellent resume distribution services to be found on the Web.

Targeted Direct Mail/Email. Three elements are critical to a successful targeted mail campaign (not mass mailing): an up-to-date mailing list, specific contact information for the hiring manager or recruiter, and follow-up action. Many job seekers have been sorely disappointed after sending out hundreds (or even thousands) of resumes to a poorly targeted and outdated list, and then compounding the error by failing to follow up by telephone or mail with each contact. Yes, each contact.

Professional or Specialized Job Search Publications. Select and subscribe to one or more of these publications which provide the inside track on positions typically advertised nowhere else. There are publications available for many career specializations, including sales, marketing, manufacturing, human resources, and so on. These publications often offer additional assistance in the areas of networking, mailing lists, and more, specific to their industry concentration.

Once you have ensured that you have a high impact, well-targeted resume in hand, it is essential to obtain strategic guidance to identify all appropriate resume distribution and networking methods at your disposal. Develop a plan, and aggressively work your plan, leaving no stone unturned in your search for job leads. Through persistent and well-planned use of as many search tools as are feasible and appropriate for you, you can produce great results, while minimizing your time and financial investment.

—*Laurie J. Smith, CPRW, IJCTC, Creative Keystrokes Executive Resume Service*

TIP #54—THE WORLD HAS GLOBALIZED

In decades past, the reality was that many people lived and worked in the same geographic region for their entire lives. Slowly, we started to move, from state to state and from coast to coast. Now, over the past 10 years, the world has globalized at a phenomenal rate with millions of people working in countries other than their own. For those with an adventurous spirit and desire to see the world, this opens unlimited employment opportunities.

Consider this . . . instead of selling industrial equipment in the midwestern United States, why not sell that same equipment in Europe, Asia, Latin America, or Africa? If you're a nurse, you can consider an assignment in a city anywhere in the world you might want to live or anywhere that needs professionals with your expertise. If you're a builder, you can build in Norway just as easily as Oregon. Your options are wide open. Just think of the opportunities, knowledge, and experience you can offer to your family!

However, international assignments are *not* for everyone. Relocating abroad does have its complications and can, indeed, be quite an adventure. You must be flexible, adaptable, resilient, and able to laugh at the unexpected in order to enjoy the experience and live comfortably in another nation.

There are basically three ways you can secure an international assignment:

1. If you're currently employed and your company has international opportunities, simply approach them to explore your options.

2. If you're not currently employed but are interested in positions overseas, approach a U.S. company and attempt to be hired here to work abroad. It is much easier to secure a job in the United States and then have the company move you to the country to which you've been assigned.

3. Apply directly to companies in the country you've chosen for relocation. This is the most difficult way to secure an international assignment, but is certainly possible and happens every day. Obviously, as with domestic relocation, you may have to travel to the location on several occasions to "close the deal."

There are many, many items you'll want to consider before relocating, including language, political stability, economic climate, tax implications, religious freedoms, schools, housing, and health care. However, most of these are the same items you would consider whether moving from Milwaukee to Toledo or Dallas to Johannesburg. Learn what you can about the culture, people, and differences in business practices. The more educated you are prior to relocating, the easier the transition will be.

For those of you who may be considering international relocation, an excellent resource for country-specific information about resumes, interviewing protocols, cultural norms, business norms, visa requirements, and much more is *The Global Resume and CV Guide* by Mary Anne Thompson. This book includes information on over 35 countries, from Chile to Russia.

—*Author's tip*

TIP #55—DON'T SURF ALL DAY LONG!

The Internet is one of today's favored job search tools and it should be. Consider all of its uses to you as a job seeker. You can:

1. Post your resume online at hundreds of websites (e.g., *www.6FigureJobs.com, www.Monster.com, www.ChiefMonster.com, www.Headhunter.net, www.JobBankUSA.com, www.NationJob. com*)

2. Search for job postings on both public and company websites

3. Submit your resume online in response to advertisements worldwide

4. Produce and distribute an online resume email campaign

5. Design your own personal website

6. Develop a CD-based career portfolio

With all of these opportunities, why would you need to do anything in your job search other than use the Internet? It seems to offer everything a job seeker could possibly need! However, that's not true. Do not allow yourself to fall into the trap of thinking that the Internet is the end-all solution. Use it wisely, and to your advantage, but do not allow it to overtake your entire job search!

Internet-based job search is just one of many activities in which you should engage when you're in the midst of an active campaign. All that you have read earlier in this chapter about networking, finding spot opportunities, working with recruiters, and more, is vital to the success of your campaign. As any successful salesperson knows, the more channels you use to get your product into the market, the more interest you generate and the more sales that you close! And remember how lucky you are—you only need one close!

Refer to pages 110–123 for a listing of some of the most useful websites for your job search campaign.

—Author's tip

TIP #56—THE RISK EXISTS

Be realistic. When you're in the market for a new position and have your resume circulating, no matter how confidentially you manage the process, you run the risk of your current employer finding out. It is a reality of today's technology-driven job search market. To minimize your risk, you must minimize your job search campaign. In some instances (e.g., a bookkeeper who is currently employed and open to better-paying positions only within her local area), keeping the job search small is the appropriate strategy.

However, this will not be the case in most circumstances. If you've made the commitment to look for a new job, you've most likely made the commitment to leave your current company. As such, you must be visible in the market. You'll have to learn to balance your search with the risk to optimize your results while maintaining your current position. This will mean a search campaign that gets your resume out to the appropriate people for the appropriate positions, while not blasting it out in thousands of emails. Use discretion and ask for confidentiality, but know that you're putting yourself in a potentially risky position.

The good news is that most employers really do expect that their employees have resumes out on the street. Any smart employee would in today's uncertain economic climate. Ten years ago, if your employer found out that you were in the market for a new job, you were most likely out the door. Fortunately, times have changed. It is no longer "the kiss of death" to have a resume circulating. Just be prepared to answer your current employer's questions about why you're searching if they should happen to find out.

Use the "Career Marketing" checklist, "Ad Response" checklist, and "Job Search Expense Journal" to help you plan, manage, and control your job search campaign.

—*Author's tip*

Web Research and Information Tools

NOTE: This list of web tools is a great start, but is by no means complete. It is highly recommended that you spend some time researching information for yourself.

Career Assessment Tools

Career Exploration	*www.experience.com*
Careerintel	*www.careerintel.com*
DISC Personality System	*www.discprofile.com*
MBTI Site	*www.typelogic.com*
Parkland College	*www.parkland.cc.il.us/ccc/planning. htm*
Personality and Career Testing	*www.w-win.com/Webb/ careerdevelopment/steps.html*
RIASEC Typology	*web.missouri.edu/~cppcwww/ holland.shtml*
Satellite Site—Many Assessment Sites	*web.missouri.edu/~cppcwww/ planlinks.shtml#assess*
Skills Testing and Certificate Site	*www.qwiz.com*

Interviewing Tips and Techniques

Dress for Success	*www.dressforsuccess.org*
Interviewing Skills	*jobsearch.about.com/business/ jobsearch/msubinterv.htm*
Introduction to Job Interviews	*www.bradleycvs.demon.co.uk/ interview/index.htm*
Job Interviews	*www.job-interview.net*
Mock Job Interview	*www1.kaplan.com/view/article/0, 1898,3134,000.html*
Northeastern University	*www.dac.neu.edu/coop. careerservices/interview.html*

Salary and Compensation Information

Abbott, Langer & Associates — *www.abbott-langer.com*

Administrative and Office Salaries — *stats.bls.gov/oco/ocos002.htm*

America's Career InfoNet — *www.acinet.org/acinet.occ_seal1.htm*

American Compensation Association — *www.acaonline.org/*

Broadcast, TV, and Radio Salaries — *www.missouri.edu/~jourvs/*

Bureau of Labor Statistics — *stats.bls.gov/ocohome.htm*

Compensation Information — *www.claytonwallis.com*

Compensationlink.com — *www.compensationlink.com*

Consultant Salaries — *www.cob.ohio-state.edu/~fin/jobs/mco/salary.htm*

Crystal Report — *www.crystalreport.com*

Economic Research Institute — *www.erieri.com*

Engineer Salaries — *fairway.ecn.purdue.edu/ESCAPE/stats/salaries.html*

JobSmart — *jobsmart.org/tools/salary/index.htm*

Medical Salaries — *www.pohly.com/salary.shtml*

MIS Salaries — *www.psrinc.com/salary.htm*

Monster.com—Negotiation Coach — *midcareer.monster.com/experts/negotiation*

Salary and Crime Calculator — *www.homefair.com/homefair/cmr/salcalc.html*

Salary Survey — *www.salarysurvey.com*

Wageweb — *www.wageweb.com*

Wall Street Journal — *careers.wsj.com/?content=cwc-salariesindex.htm*

Working Woman — *www.workingwoman.com/salary*

Dictionaries and Glossaries

Acronyms	*acronymfinder.com*
Biotechnology Dictionary	*biotechterms.org/sourcebook/index. phtml*
Business Glossary	*washingtonpost.com/wp-srv/business/ longterm/glossary/index.htm*
Canadian English to American English Dictionary	*www.luther.bc.ca/~dave7cnv/ cdnspelling/cdnspelling.html*
Computer Acronymns	*cramsession.brainbuzz.com/ studytips/acronyms_list.asp*
Computer Industry Dictionary	*wombat.doc.ic.ac.uk/foldoc/index. html*
Computer Industry Glossary	*www.webopedia.com*
Duhaime's Law Dictionary	*www.wwlia.org/diction.htm*
Educational Dictionary/ Thesaurus	*www.wordsmyth.net*
English-Spanish Glossary	*technoguia.wcom.com/english/index. html*
Foreign Language Translation	*www.altavista.com*
Grammar and Style	*ww.drawing.oregon.edu/~uopubs/ grammar/grammar.html#top*
High-Tech Dictionary	*www.computeruser.com/resources/ dictionary/dictionary.html*
Investment Dictionary	*www.county.com.au/web/webdict. nsf/pages/index?open*
Investment Industry Dictionary	*www.investorwords.com/g1.htm*
Legal Dictionary	*www.nolo.com/dictionary/ dictionary_topic_listing.cfm? Category=6*
Legal Dictionary	*www.wwlia.org/diction.htm*
Legal Industry Glossary	*www.law.com*

Merriam-Webster College Dictionary and Thesaurus	*www.m-w.com/home.htm*
Online Chat Language Dictionary	*www.currents.net/resources/ dictionary/chat.html*
Restaurant Industry Glossary	*www.restaurantreport.com/index. html*
TechEncyclopedia	*www.techweb.com/encyclopedia/*
Technology Terms Dictionary	*www.currents.net/resources/ dictionary*
Telecommunications Glossary	*bellatlantic.com/wholesale/html/res_ glossary_l.htm*
The Virtual Reference Desk— Dictionaries	*bigdog.lib.purdue.edu/vlibrary/ reference/dict.html*
WhatIs?com Technology Terms	*www.whatis.com*
WordWeb	*www.wordweb.co/uk/free/*

Job Search Sites

6 Figure Jobs	*www.6figurejobs.com*
Accounting Careers	*www.CPAnet.com*
Accounting Careers	*www.aafa.com*
Accounting Careers	*www.accountingnet.com*
Acting Careers	*www.playbill.com/playbill/*
Acting Careers	*www.auditions.com*
Adams Online	*www.adamsonline.com*
Advertising Careers	*www.adweek.com*
Agricultural Careers	*www.agricareers.com*
America's Job Bank	*www.ajb.dni.us/*
Architecture Careers	*www.aia.org*
Automotive Careers	*www.autocareers.com*
Aviation Careers	*www.findapilot.com*
Best Jobs	*www.bestjobsusa.com*
Biotechnology Careers	*www.chemistry.com*

Biotechnology Careers	*www.medsearch.com*
Career Atlas for the Road	*isdn.net/nis/*
Career Builder	*www.careerbuilder.com*
Career Central	*www.careercentral.com*
Career City	*www.careercity.com*
Career Engine	*www.careerengine.com*
Career Exchange	*www.careerexchange.com*
Career Exposure	*www.careerexposure.com*
Career Magazine	*www.careermag.com/*
Career Mosaic	*www.careermosaic.com/*
Career Path	*www.careerpath.com/*
Career Shop	*www.careershop.com/*
Career Site	*www.careersite.com*
Career Web	*www.cweb.com/*
Career Web	*www.careerweb.com*
Careers	*www.career.com*
Careers	*www.jobsonline.com*
Careers	*MyJobSearch.com*
Careers	*www.theworksite.com*
Careers	*www.workseek.com*
Careers for Minorities	*www.minorities-jb.com*
Careers for Minorities	*www.blackworld.com*
Careers for Seniors	*www.maturityworks.org*
Careers for Women	*www.womenconnect.com/info/career/index.htm*
Careers for Women	*www.classifiedsforwomen.com*
CEO Careers	*www.ceoexpress.com*
CFO Careers	*www.cfonet.com*
Construction Careers	*www.pubworks.org*
Construction Careers	*www.hardhatsonline.com*
Education Careers	*www.petersons.com*

Education Careers	*www.case.org*
Educational Careers	*www.careerage.com*
Educational Careers	*chronicle.com/jobs*
Educational Careers	*www.jobs.edunet.com*
Educational Careers	*www.educationjobs.com*
Educational Careers	*www.edweek.org/jobs.cfm*
Educational Careers	*www.education-world.com/jobs*
Educational Careers	*www.hire-ed.org*
Educational Careers	*www.iteachnet.com/jobsb.html*
Educational Careers	*www.iqmedia.co.uk*
Educational Careers	*www.academic360.com*
Educational Careers	*www.teaching-jobs.org/index.htm*
Educational Careers	*www.ujobbank.com*
Employment—General	*employment.digitalcity.com*
Engineering Careers	*www.engineeringjobs.com*
Engineering Careers	*www.ieee.org/jobs.html*
Engineering Careers	*www.nspe.org*
Engineering Careers	*www.ideasjn.com*
Entry-Level Careers	*www.collegegrad.com*
Entry-Level Careers	*www.gradseek.com*
Entry-Level Careers	*www.campuscareercenter.com*
Entry-Level Careers	*www.jobtrak.com*
Environmental Careers	*www.ecojobs.com*
Environmental Careers	*www.empty.net*
Environmental Careers	*www.environmental-jobs.com*
Excite—Find a Job	*www.excite.com*
Fashion Careers	*www.fashioncareercenter.com*
FedWorld	*www.fedworld.gov/*
Finance Careers	*www.financeseek.com*
Finance Careers	*www.careerbank.com*
Finance Careers	*www.cfonet.com*

Flip Dog	*www.flipdog.com*
Food Service Careers	*www.escoffier.com*
Food Service Careers	*www.foodservice.com*
Food Service Careers	*www.chefsatwork.com*
Food Service Careers	*www.pastrywiz.com*
Food Service Careers	*www.culinary.com*
Food Service Careers	*www.webfoodpros.com*
For Work	*www.4work.com*
FutureStep	*www.futurestep.com*
Get a Job	*www.getajob.com/*
Global Job Shop	*www.globaljobshop.com*
Government Careers	*www.fedjobs.com*
Government Careers	*www.jobsingovernment.com*
Government Careers	*www.getagovjob.com*
Headhunter Net	*www.headhunter.net/jobs/*
Health Care Careers	*www.healthjobsite.com*
Health Care Careers	*www.HealthLeaders.com*
Health Care Careers	*www.gvpub.com*
Health Care Careers	*www.jobspan.com*
Health Care Careers	*www.rehabjobs.com*
Health Care Careers	*www.healthcareers-online.com*
Health Insurance Careers	*www.ehealthinsurance.com*
Help Wanted	*www.helpwanted.com/*
Hot Jobs	*www.hotjobs.com*
Human Resource Careers	*www.hrhub.com*
Human Resource Careers	*www.hrjobs.com*
Human Resource Careers	*www.jobs4hr.com*
Human Resource Careers	*www.shrm.org*
Human Resource Careers	*www.empty.net*
Insurance Careers	*www.rollinssearch.com*
Insurance Careers	*www.connectyou.com*

Insurance Careers	www.insweb.com
International Careers	www.latpro.com
International Careers	www.overseasjobs.com
International Careers	www.escapeartist.com
International Careers	www.internationaljobs.com
International Careers	www.mediainfo.com
International Careers	www.hoovers.com
Internet Resume Center	www.inpursuit.com/sirc/
It's Your Job Now	www.ItsYourJobNow.com
Job Bank USA	www.jobbankusa.com
Job Center	www.jobcenter.com
Job Exchange	www.jobexchange.com
Job Locator	www.joblocator.com
Job Market	www.thejobmarket.com
Job Options	www.joboptions.com
Job Source (entry level)	www.jobsource.com
Job Track	www.jobtrak.com
Job Web	www.jobweb.com
JobNet	www.jobnet.com
Journalism/Broadcasting Careers	www.mediaweek.com/classifieds/multi.asp
Journalism/Broadcasting Careers	www.tvjobs.com
Journalism/Broadcasting Careers	www.airwaves.com
Legal Careers	www.finelaw.com
Legal Careers	www.greedyassociates.com
Legal Careers	www.emplawyer.net
Legal Careers	www.seamless.com/jobs
Legal Careers	www.legalemploym.com
Library Careers	www.zoots.com/libjob/jefflee.com

Logistics Careers	*www.jobsinlogistics.com*
Manufacturing Careers	*www.edmondspersonnel.com*
Manufacturing Careers	*www.raijobs.com*
Marketing Careers	*www.marketingjobs.com*
Marketing Careers	*www.ama.org*
MBA Careers	*www.mbajob.com*
MBA Careers	*www.mrinet.com*
MBA Careers	*www.mbacareers.com*
MBA Employment Connection	*www.mbanetwork.com/meca*
Medical Careers	*www.medhunters.com*
Medical Careers	*www.medsearch.com*
Medical Careers	*www.NHRphysician.com*
Medical Careers	*www.webmd.com*
Medical Careers	*www.medwebplus.com*
Medical Recruiters and Search Firms	*www.medhunters.com*
Medzilla (for Medical and Related Jobs)	*www.medzilla.com/*
Monster Board	*www.monster.com*
Multimedia Careers	*www.salley.com*
Nation Jobs	*www.nationjob.com*
Net Temps	*www.net-temps.com*
Nursing Careers	*www.nursingspectrum.com*
Nursing Careers	*www.nursesnetwork.com*
Nursing Careers	*www.nursingcenter.com*
Online Jobs	*www.online-jobs.com*
Pharmaceutical Careers	*www.drugstore.com*
Pharmaceutical Jobs	*www.coreynahman.com/ pharmaceutical_company_database. html*
Physician Careers	*www.physemp.com*

Professional Careers—All Industries	*www.vault.com*
Professional Careers—All Industries	*www.professionalcareer.com*
Quality Engineering Careers	*www.quality.org*
Quality Engineering Careers	*www.asq.com*
Retail Careers	*www.retailseek.com*
Retail Careers	*www.retailjobnet.com*
Sales Careers	*www.salesseek.com*
Science Careers	*www.chemistry.mond.org*
Science Careers	*www.ggrweb.com/job.htm*
Science Careers	*www.aps.org/industry.htm*
Social Work Careers	*www.impactonline.com*
Social Work Careers	*www.socialservice.com*
Technology Careers	*www.ceweekly.com*
Technology Careers	*www.dice.com*
Technology Careers	*www.GeekSeek.com*
Technology Careers	*www.atb.org*
Technology Careers	*www.computerjobs.com*
Technology Careers	*www.techies.com*
Technology Careers	*www.jobserve.com*
Technology Careers	*www.passportacces.com*
Technology Careers	*www.careershop.com*
Technology Careers	*taps.com*
Technology Careers	*www.computerwork.com*
Technology Careers	*www.selectjobs.com*
Technology Careers	*it.jobsearch.org*
Technology Careers	*www.brainbuzz.com*
Technology Careers	*www.computerworld.com*
Technology Careers	*www.beardsleygroup.com*
Technology Careers	*www.chancellor.com*

Technology Careers	www.computerwork.com
Technology Careers	www.justtechjobs.com
Technology Careers	www.psisearch.com
Technology Careers	www.techsource.org
Technology Careers	www.telecommunications.com
Technology Careers (Contract)	www.ntes.com
Top Jobs	www.topjobsusa.com
Transportation Careers	www.truckers.com
Transportation Careers	www.jobxchange.com
Work Tree	www.worktree.com
Yahoo Careers	www.yahoo.com/Business_and_Economy/Employment/Jobs

Company Information

AllBusiness.com	www.comfind.com
America's Employers	www.americasemployers.com
Big Book Electronic Yellow Pages	www.bigbook.com
Business Directory Information	www.555-1212.com
Chambers of Commerce	www.uschamber.com/mall/states.htm
Fortune 500 Companies	www.fortune.com/fortune/fortune500
Global Business-to-Business Communications	www.vault.com/vstore/lists/companylist.cfm
Industry Information	home.sprintmail.com/~debflanagan/index.html
Information About Key Executives	www.edgar-online.com
Intellifact.com	www.intellifact.com/company_research.htm

Hoover's Business Profiles	*www.hoovers.com/*
New World of Work	*www.experiencenetwork.com/ newsite/comp_center/index.html*
Small Business Information	*www.infousa.com*
Technology Company Information	*www.corptech.com/index.cfm*
WetFeet.com	*www.wetfeet.com/asp/ companyresource_home.asp*

U.S. Government Websites

Daily News Site for Federal Employees, Managers, and Executives	*www.govexec.com*
Detailed Information About the Federal Personnel System	*www.opm.gov*
Good General Information and Links	*www.federaljobs.net*
Information and For-Fee Automated Emailings	*www.hrsjobs.com*
Information on Thrift Savings Plan	*www.tsp.gov*
Job Application Information	*www.fedjobs.com*
Listing of Job Vacancies	*www.usajobs.opm.gov*
News Happening—U.S. Federal Government	*www.planetgov.com*
Users QuickHire Software for Filing Applications Online	*www.usgs.gov*

Professional Careers and Employment Associations

| American Bar Association— Employment Law | *www.abanet.org* |

American College of Healthcare Executives	*www.ache.org*
American Compensation Association	*www.acaonline.org*
American Counseling Association	*www.counseling.org*
American National Career Development Association	*www.ncda.org*
American Psychological Association	*www.apa.org*
American Society of Association Executives	*www.asanet.org*
Association for Internet Recruiting	*www.recruitersnetwork.com*
Association of Career Management Consulting Firms International	*www.aocfi.org*
British Columbia HR Management Association	*www.bchrma.org*
Canadian Compensation Association	*www.cca-acr.org*
Career Masters Institute	*www.cminstitute.com*
Career Research and Testing	*www.careertrainer.com*
College of Healthcare Information Management Executives	*www.cio-chime.org*
Five O'Clock Club	*www.fiveoclockclub.com*
Home-Based Working Moms	*www.hbwm.com*
Home Business Works	*www.homebusinessworks.com*
HR Research Association	*www.Humrro.org*
Institute of Personnel and Development (UK)	*www.ipd.co.uk*

International Association of Administrative Professionals	*www.iaap-hq.org*
International Association of Career Management Professionals	*www.iacmp.org*
International Board for Career Management Certification	*www.iacmp.org/cmcindex.html*
International Coach Federation	*www.coachfederation.org*
Jobs for America's Graduates	*www.jag.org*
National Association of Colleges and Employers	*www.jobweb.org*
National Association of Temporary and Staffing Services	*www.natss.com*
National Board of Certified Counselors Inc.	*www.nbcc.org*
National Resume Writers Association	*www.nrwa.com*
Professional Association of Resume Writers	*www.parw.com*
Professional Resume Writing and Research Association	*www.prwra.com*
Recruiters Online Network	*www.ipa.com*
Society for HR Management	*www.shrm.org*

—Author's tip

CAREER MARKETING CHECKLIST

Directions: Use the following checklist to keep track of all of your job search and career marketing activities. Check off each item as you have completed it, fill in the names of specific companies or services that you've used (as indicated), and be sure to note renewal dates.

IMPORTANT NOTE: Not all of the job search techniques listed here are appropriate for every job seeker. What strategies you use will depend on your specific objectives for type of position, geographic preference, and salary requirements.

———— **NETWORKING** ————
Round 1: ————————————
Round 2: ————————————
Round 3: ————————————
Round 4: ————————————
Round 5: ————————————

———— **TARGETED DIRECT MAIL/EMAIL—COMPANIES** ————
Company 1: ———————————— (Renewal: ———)
Company 2: ———————————— (Renewal: ———)

———— **TARGETED DIRECT MAIL/EMAIL—RECRUITERS** ————
Company 1: ———————————— (Renewal: ———)
Company 2: ———————————— (Renewal: ———)

———— **TARGETED DIRECT MAIL/EMAIL—**
VENTURE CAPITAL FIRMS ————
Company 1: ———————————— (Renewal: ———)
Company 2: ———————————— (Renewal: ———)

———— **SUBSCRIPTIONS TO JOB LEAD REPORTS** ————
Company 1: ———————————— (Renewal: ———)
Company 2: ———————————— (Renewal: ———)

INTERNET RESUME POSTING SERVICES

Company 1: _____ (Renewal: _____)

Company 2: _____ (Renewal: _____)

Company 3: _____ (Renewal: _____)

Company 4: _____ (Renewal: _____)

Company 5: _____ (Renewal: _____)

Company 6: _____ (Renewal: _____)

INTERVIEW TRAINING/COACHING

Company 1: _____

Company 2: _____

AD RESPONSE CHECKLIST

Directions: Use this checklist to keep track of all of the responses you send to print and online advertisements.

Job Title: _____

Company/Recruiter Name: _____

Address: _____

Email: _____ Website: _____

Phone: _____ Fax: _____

Source: _____

Date of Initial Response: _____

Date for Follow-Up: _____

Additional Notes: _____

_____

_____

_____

Job Title: _____

Company/Recruiter Name: _____

Address: _____

Email: _____ Website: _____

Phone: _____ Fax: _____

Source: _____

Date of Initial Response: _____

Date for Follow-Up: _____

Additional Notes: _____

_____

_____

_____

Job Title: _____

Company/Recruiter Name: _____

Address: _____

Email: _____ Website: _____

Phone: _____ Fax: _____

Source: _____

Date of Initial Response: _____

Date for Follow-Up: _____

Additional Notes: _____

_____

_____

_____

Job Title: _____

Company/Recruiter Name: _____

Address: _____

Email: _____ Website: _____

Phone: _____ Fax: _____

Source: _____

Date of Initial Response: _____

Date for Follow-Up: _____

Additional Notes: _____

_____

_____

_____

Job Title: _____

Company/Recruiter Name: _____

Address: _____

Email: _____ Website: _____

Phone: _____ Fax: _____

Source: _____

Date of Initial Response: _____

Date for Follow-Up: _____

Additional Notes: _____

_____

_____

_____

JOB SEARCH EXPENSE JOURNAL

NOTE: Job search expenses are ONLY tax deductible if you are looking for a position in your same field. If you are changing professions, expenses are NOT deductible. It is highly recommended that you consult an accountant to determine which of the following, if any, are tax deductible in your particular situation.

DATE   ITEM   COST

DATE   ITEM   COST

DATE   ITEM   COST

DATE   ITEM   COST

DATE   ITEM   COST

DATE   ITEM   COST

DATE   ITEM   COST

DATE   ITEM   COST

DATE   ITEM   COST

DATE   ITEM   COST

DATE   ITEM   COST

DATE   ITEM   COST

DATE   ITEM   COST

DATE   ITEM   COST

DATE   ITEM   COST

CHAPTER 5

Optimizing Your Networking Skills, Performance, and Success

TIP #57—WHAT DOES NETWORKING REALLY MEAN?

If you closely examine the word *networking,* you'll discover its true meaning:

N = Nerve. Your network will give you the nerve and the courage to do something different, more interesting, more fun, and more exciting in your career and your life.

E = Energy. Your network will provide you with the energy, drive, and enthusiasm so vital to a successful job search and a lifelong career of personal and professional fulfillment.

T = Trust. Trust is the foundation upon which you must build your network and what will catapult it into the future.

W = Work. Don't ever forget that networking is work! There is a purpose and a mission to networking—a new position and life-long career progression.

O = Opportunities. Your network will open the door to new career opportunities, today and in the future.

R = Relationships. The underlying themes of networking are re-lationship development and lifelong relationship management.

K = Knowledge. Knowledge is the greatest gift you'll receive from your network—knowledge about new careers, new jobs, and new professional opportunities that are waiting for you.

Understand and appreciate the power of your network and your results can be extraordinary!

—Author's tip

TIP #58—THREE IMPORTANT RULES OF NETWORKING

1. Networking is the single most successful strategy for job search and lifelong career management. There is no other ac-tivity you can engage in that will provide more resources, contacts, or opportunities. Therefore, it must be at the fore-front of all of your career management efforts throughout your lifetime, not just during an active job search.

2. When you are networking, *never* ask anyone for a job! This is critical. When you contact your network, ask for their help. People are more than willing to help you, give you ideas, and even make contacts on your behalf. Most, however, don't have a job for you and don't want to be asked. What you want from them are other contacts, referrals, and doors to be opened.

3. Virtually no one likes to network. Unfortunately, that really doesn't matter. What does matter is that you get out and do it!

—Author's tip

TIP #59—THE DOMINO EFFECT

Once you've arrived at the "do-it" stage in job search, tell others about your goal to search for a new job. If others are continually asking about your progress, you'll be more committed. One hundred percent of all people looking for jobs feel that they are alone in this endeavor; but that's not true. There are people out there who want to help and who can help you. What's more, these people and resources are usually quite easy to access. All you have to do is contact them. Here are the tricks:

- Begin by telling everyone in your immediate and extended family that you're looking for a job or a career change. Most job seekers tell their immediate family but don't call grandparents, cousins, aunts and uncles, or distant relatives. Most family members, even distant ones, are happy to help a relative. Call them! Email them! Write them!

- Call former coworkers and tell them that you'd like to make a job change. People who once worked with you are in a great position to "sing your praises" to other prospective employers.

- Plan an informal get-together with good friends and tell them about your search. This type of comfortable setting can help get a brainstorming conversation started. Take notes and follow up on leads, even if those leads don't seem likely to produce results.

- Contact any former professors or teachers with whom you may have stayed in contact.

- List all your extra activities. When you attend these activities (meetings, social outings, sporting events, etc.), let people there know you're looking for a new position. You will be surprised at the ideas you get from people you associate with in your spare time. For example, I served as president of a local service organization's board of directors. These 35 people are lawyers, bankers, real estate agents, business owners—you get the picture. They travel in many circles and can get my name mentioned in places I would never go.

- Tell professionals who deliver services to you. This includes your doctor, child care provider, pharmacist, and the grocer who always asks how you're doing.

- Be patient. Finding the right fit takes time. Becoming impatient leaves room for error in judgment. Wait for an opportunity that fits your career objective.

The above triggers the "domino effect." Why does it work in the first place?

- People want to help other people. Allow them to do so. Remember to send a thank-you note to any person who tries to help you, even if his or her help doesn't result in an interview or an offer. You want to create goodwill and continued willingness by people to help you.

- The more people you tell the wider your net and the more likely you'll uncover an opportunity.

Gather your resources and you will not only gain support, but you will develop resources about careers and opportunities you might not have found on your own. If you are shopping for a comfortable pair of walking shoes, would you go to only 1 or 2 stores, or would you go to a mall where you have 23 stores to choose from? Sharing your job search with others is analogous: Your chance of finding the right shoes (or a great job) are increased!

—*Barb Poole, CPRW, Hire Imaging*

TIP #60—BUILDING YOUR NETWORK FOR SUCCESS

The most powerful tool in your career-building toolkit is your network. Ideally, you have a terrific network in place, so that you can draw on it when you want to advance in your company, change your career track, or find a great new job.

Realistically, though, you may feel like some of my clients who say, "I have no network. . . . I am not the networking type. . . . All of my contacts are in other cities. . . . I cannot call people I have not talked to in years. . . . I feel like I am begging. . . . I have never had to beg for a job in my life. The jobs just come to me."

I always answer, "You do have a network and you can be an effective networker." Here's how: Networking, when done properly, produces outstanding results. It is about wanting to help people, who, in turn, want to help you. Often people associate the "social butterfly" with a networker. We have all had these shallow encounters and cannot wait for the butterfly to flit away and pollinate another flower. These folks are not networking. They are playing. Networking is work.

Let us look at the work involved in building and maintaining your powerful network.

Step 1. Be clear about your goal. Name the job you want and identify the companies that interest you.

Step 2. Write down the names of all the people you know. Include former managers, colleagues, competitors, vendors, alumni, professional association members, community and church leaders, realtors, your dentist, doctor, accountant, and pest control specialist. You get the picture.

Everyone you know is a potential resource. Do not let the fact that you have not been in contact for 3, 5, or even 20 years deter you.

One of my clients, Joe, had never networked before, but agreed to give it a try. He was clear about his goal of becoming a national sales manager for a mid-sized security technology firm. In the process of calling everyone he knew, he decided to contact his pest control specialist. The guy said, "I have a friend who runs a security technology company. They are successful and growing. I bet they could use you. I'll call and tell him to expect your call."

Joe is now negotiating his salary and benefit package for the national sales manager role with that company.

Step 3. Educate your network contacts and invite them to educate you about their needs. Remember a network consists of mutually beneficial relationships. Interview your contacts to be sure you understand their needs and goals, and then ask, "How can I help? What contacts would be helpful?" Give them referrals.

In turn, tell them about your goal, target companies, credentials, and transferable skills. Ask for at least two contacts. You might say, "Can you identify two people who might know someone in the XYZ industry who could use my background and skills?"

When you receive their names and phone numbers, ask, "May I use your name?" or "Do you think it will be difficult to get through the secretary to reach her?" If the person says yes, then ask if they would do you the favor of calling their contact to say you will be calling. The beauty of this process is that your network contact presells you.

With each secondary contact, use the name of the person referring you. Deliver a powerful 90-second commercial highlighting your goal, credentials, skills, and achievements. Ask for a referral to two other people who might be able to use your skills and experience. This approach does not put the secondary contact on the spot, yet it leaves the door open for him or her to interview you more closely.

During an active job campaign, make at least 20 of these calls each day. Write the number 20 on a Post-it note and put it on your mirror or refrigerator. Schedule the time for the calls on your daily planner.

Step 4. Write a thank-you note to everyone who helps you.

Step 5. When you are invited to a networking function, take plenty of business cards. On arrival, walk up to the host, introduce yourself, thank him for the invitation, and ask for an introduction to five people who might be able to assist you. By virtue of the introduction, the host adds to your credibility. Ask each contact for a business card, listen to their needs, and make notes on the back of the card.

Give each person two of your cards, saying, "One for you and one to pass along." Follow up with each contact.

Step 6. During an aggressive search campaign, consider invoking the "three-yard rule." I learned this strategy from Ona Brown, the daughter of the well-known motivational speaker, Les Brown. Tell everyone within three yards of you what you are seeking.

Ona used this in New York City when she was looking for an apartment near mid-town Manhattan. She said, "I'm new to the area. I'm looking for an apartment and can afford a monthly rent of $1000."

One day at a concert, she was washing her hands in the ladies' room. She saw a woman at the next sink, thought why not, and invoked the "three-yard rule." The woman said, "I don't have anything, but I have a friend who might." She arranged an introduction.

Ona got the apartment of her dreams at the price she wanted to pay. Seasoned New Yorkers said it could not be done within three months of arrival in the city. The "three-yard rule" proved them wrong.

Nick, a client, used the rule on the phone during a call from a well-respected environmental group soliciting votes for a mayoral candidate. Nick said, "Yes, I will go out to vote. In fact, I am involved in a career change into environmental advocacy. How can I get to know the local, state, and national leaders?"

The volunteer on the other end of the line said, "Come in and volunteer for the get-out-to-vote campaign, and I will personally introduce you to the local and state leadership. They will then get you to the national leaders." My client volunteered on the spot.

Step 7. Ask. Statistically, 90 percent do not ask for what they want. An excellent salesperson once said to me, "You won't get the sale unless you ask for the order."

Step 8. As the Nike slogan says, "Just do it." Networking is not an innate skill. It is developed through practice. You do not need to be an outgoing type to be successful. Some of the most effective networkers I know are quiet, somewhat reserved individuals. They are effective because they care and return the favor when asked.

—*Kathleen McInerney, CEIP, JCTC, Career Edge, Inc.*

TIP #61—ENERGIZE YOUR SEARCH—JOIN A JOB CLUB

Job clubs have been around for many years and given the present job market, the need has now increased substantially. Anyone can join a club—individuals re-entering the job market, those who have been downsized, career changers, people working for a promotion, individuals who simply want to change jobs and re-energize their careers . . . anyone.

Effective job clubs offer a place for job seekers to meet regularly to discuss their efforts, success stories, obstacles, employment leads, and referrals. In addition, today's job clubs are becoming more of an educational forum, rather than just a way for job seekers to swap employment leads and discuss individual concerns. The effectiveness of the club increases by focusing on teaching job seekers to properly prepare for their search. Some may offer workshops on resume writing, cover letters, interviewing techniques, job search skills, and follow-up strategies. Many will have informative presentations given by guest speakers including employers, employment professionals, career training counselors, assessment specialists, and successful job seekers who share their experiences and insights.

The benefits of job clubs are incredible. Job seekers will:

- Quickly be able to start and enjoy their search
- Uncover their transferable, adaptive, and job-related skills
- Learn how their weaknesses and strengths affect their career success
- Learn how to correctly market themselves, both in writing and in person
- Uncover what employers are looking for in employees
- Stay focused and motivated on their search campaigns
- No longer feel isolated and depressed
- Make lots of new contacts
- Find a new position faster

Each job club is structured differently; it is wise to ask questions prior to committing yourself. You may be able to speak to present members and hear some first-hand testimonials and success stories. Make sure you know what services the club provides, when they meet, and if they offer workshops and guest speakers. If you are unable to find a local club, search the Internet and consider joining an online/virtual job club. Be forewarned however. If a job club requests a sizable upfront investment, look elsewhere.

Don't miss out on this chance to get motivated, use creative strategies, build self-confidence, and jump-start your search. Prepare for your first meeting by dressing professionally and bringing one or two job leads to share with the group. It is important to understand that a job club is "give and take," not just "take," so be prepared to share information. There is something to be said about using the *team* approach—"*Together Each Achieves More.*"

—*Candace Davies, BBA, CPRW, Cando Career Coaching &*
Resume Writing

TIP #62—FIND A PARTNER

If, for whatever reason, joining a job club just doesn't work for you, then consider finding a job search partner.

Going it alone is tough, even with the support of your family and friends. It will be of immeasurable value to you to partner with another individual in the midst of a job search so that you can support one another and not feel that you are so isolated. What's even better is to partner with someone who is in the same or a similar industry and profession to yours, thereby increasing the chances that each of you will find a great new opportunity, even if you find it for each other.

Job search partners are great. When you partner you accomplish several things:

- *You have someone to whom you are accountable.* If you've told your partner that you were going to make 10 new contacts this week, then you'd better do so. Don't let your partner down; you don't want to be let down.

- *You have someone to share the experience with.* There are many ups and downs in job search. If you can find someone to share those with, it will significantly reduce your stress and frustration.

- *You can help each other solve problems and overcome obstacles.* When you share difficult experiences, work-related issues, and other things negatively impeding the success of your search, you and your partner can significantly reduce the impact of those items.

- *You can share job leads.* With two of you working on similar campaigns, there will be close to twice the number of leads and opportunities.

- *You can split the research.* Researching job leads, company contact information, recruiter names, and more can be time consuming. If you share these tasks with your partner, it will significantly reduce the amount of time each of you has to devote to this effort and double the amount of your research findings.

- *You can provide referrals.* It may be that you interviewed for a position and, whether your decision or the company's, there just isn't a match. Pass this opportunity along to your partner and perhaps it may be right for him.

—*Author's tip*

TIP #63—Stay in Touch with Your Recruiter Network

Keep . . . your networking working, and your eyes and ears open for clues of changes coming that could be hazardous to the health of your career. Never stop looking out for number one.

—Harvey Mackay, *Sharkproof*

After 14 years in the recruiting business, I'm often amazed at the lack of forethought and planning that goes into individuals' careers. By far I would say a majority of folks employ an emergency career management strategy: I need another job because of a layoff; I have to move fast because the company's going in the wrong direction; I'm desperate to leave because I'm dying here! With the demise of corporate loyalty to employees over the last 20 years, and the frenetic fall of dot-coms on every e-corner, the phrase "job security" has become an oxymoron. The time has come for working individuals to keep their options open—always open.

How does one focus on a job, while at the same time staying abreast of new opportunities? The answer is simple: You must establish "career partnerships" with professional recruiters.

Here's a quick test to determine if you use the proven strategies and tactics for Lifetime Career Management. Let's say you just landed a great position (on your own or through a headhunter), making more money than you ever have, doing exactly what you want to do. Which of these do you handle the first week on the job?

A. Notify everyone involved in your search that you're happy and settled now, so please "take me off your list."

B. Update your resume to include your present job description and send it along with an updated "wish list" to your favorite recruiter(s).

C. Find the nearest dry cleaner and Starbucks to the office.

A is the current standard. B sounds absurd, but let me make a case for executing it—even before C. If you don't update your career partners/recruiters right away, you will only remember to do so during your next desperate moment. That is emergency career management. You do it now not because you're already available to make another move, nor will you post your new resume everywhere (e.g., the Internet). Yet, putting it immediately in the hands of a few trusted recruiters who know your long-term hopes and desires keeps you tuned in to opportunities that you should at least know about . . . which you won't if you "check out."

Besides the short-term benefits of affiliating with search professionals (getting a job now), there are long-term rewards for life! Just as the Hollywood celebrity and sports types can focus on what they do best by having someone else manage their career movement, a few chosen career partners can support your long-term goals and desires. This only happens when you stay connected with your recruiters, not by waiting until you need to make an emergency move. My advice is to always, always, always keep your eyes and ears open. Keep your contact information current and your resume and wish list continually updated.

I respect your loyalty to a company that continues to provide the opportunities and compensation you deserve. Respect yourself enough to always have a secret agent informing you of whether they are doing so—or not. When you find those headhunters you can hold as "family career doctors," stay tuned in. You could be very surprised at what they might uncover for you over the long run. Though you may not move for another 3, 5, or 10 years, it doesn't hurt to hear about what's going on in your field. Pay attention to what's out there—you never know when it might be you!

> Take a chance on romance. Even if you're secure in your job and not seeking to make a switch, you may change your mind if the right opportunity comes along. If a recruiter offers you a discreet interview with someone who has expressed an interest in you, consider exploring the jungle. You could be pleasantly surprised.

—Harvey Mackay, *Sharkproof*

—*Darrell W. Gurney, CPC, JCTC, A Permanent Success National Career Coaching & Search Partners*

TIP #64—MANAGING YOUR NETWORK FOR LIFE

Networking is a lifelong process that should begin at the earliest point in your career (e.g., high school graduation, college graduation, first job) and continue on forever.

Picture your career as a winding path through a magnificent rainforest. As you travel along, you stop to collect things. In the rainforest, you might pick up an unusual rock formation or a beautiful plant. In your career, you pick up people—people that you work with, buy from, sell to, partner with, and have any other type of relationship with. You pick them up and keep them close to you should you ever need them in the future or should they ever need you. (Always remember, networking is a reciprocal relationship!)

To optimize your career success, keep your network fluid, dynamic, and constantly growing as you meet new people, form new associations, and develop new business and personal relationships. Networking is evolutionary, changing with you over the entire span of your career. Most importantly, it is one of your most valuable assets, for it is your network that will offer you the greatest future opportunities and most powerful new relationships.

Use the Network Contact Log on the next page to keep track of all your contacts and the appropriate follow-up action for each.

—Author's tip

NETWORK CONTACT LOG

NAME _____ REFERRED BY _____

COMPANY NAME _____

ADDRESS _____

PHONE _____ FAX _____ EMAIL _____

NOTES: _____

_____

_____

_____

NAME _____ REFERRED BY _____

COMPANY NAME _____

ADDRESS _____

PHONE _____ FAX _____ EMAIL _____

NOTES: _____

_____

_____

_____

NAME _____ REFERRED BY _____

COMPANY NAME _____

ADDRESS _____

PHONE _____ FAX _____ EMAIL _____

NOTES: _____

_____

_____

_____

CHAPTER 6

Interviewing and Winning the Offer

TIP #65—INTERVIEW STRATEGIES THAT WORK

Almost everyone, at one time or another, has had an interview which did not go well. Many job seekers end up wearing a T-shirt that says "I came. I interviewed. I didn't get the job." To increase your chances of being hired, follow these 10 steps before, during, and after your next job interview, and you will be a more confident job seeker.

Before the Interview

1. *Research the organization.* Research the organization, the job in general, and its salary norms. Failing to do this makes you an uninformed applicant and you'll be disregarded as a serious candidate. Researching a potential employer helps you make a favorable impression. Companies like to know you've

taken the time to learn something about their structure, history, products, services, sales, financial soundness, trends, competition, and so on. Doing this also facilitates your ability to ask insightful questions, another opportunity to score big points. Get the scoop through networking contacts, business directories, trade journals, newspapers, the Internet, or even the person who answers the phone.

2. *Review your resume.* Your resume should be perfect. A resume creates an image of who you are and what you're about. The experience should show a prospective employer what you accomplished rather than a mere list of duties and credentials. Some questions will certainly be based on your resume's content so be sure you can talk about every single item on your resume. Remember, it's often what got you the interview in the first place.

3. *Practice.* Don't be caught off guard. Check out several job search books at the library or a bookstore for a few of the most frequently asked interview questions. Given enough interview scenarios you're bound to be asked a few of these. Therefore, it makes good sense to practice your answers. This will increase your anticipatory prowess, and your confidence will soar.

4. *Prepare a list of questions you can ask.* Remember interviewing is a two-way street. You're entitled to ask questions, so ask away, but be prepared. The kinds of questions you ask can, and often do, make a significant impression on your interviewer and can distinguish you from the competition. Questions could include information about a typical day on the job, what challenges your predecessor faced in the same position, the largest problem that the staff and/or department is currently dealing with, the company's 5- and 10-year plans, and more.

The Day of the Interview

5. *Dress and adjust your attitude for success.* Give yourself a "once over" before you arrive. It's trite but true: First impressions

count and you won't have a second chance to make a first impression.

6. *Manage your time wisely.* Plan your trip so that you arrive at the interview approximately 10 minutes early (no earlier). Realize that the interview starts the minute you arrive, even if you must wait in the lobby before the actual meeting.

During the Interview

7. *Follow the lead of the interviewer.* The interviewer generally sets the pace and tone of the interview. But, remember that it's fine to be deliberate with your answers. Take a minute and think before you respond. If you suspect the interviewer is struggling with her role, try to keep the conversation going without dominating the interview. It might comfort you a bit to know that it can be just as uncomfortable on the other side of the desk!

8. *Determine the next step.* Don't leave the interview without inquiring about the next step. You'll only feel frustrated if you don't know what to expect in the future. Ask the employer when a hiring decision will be made. Will you be contacted or should you call back on a certain day? If you're convinced you would be a perfect fit for the job, say so before you leave. If you want the job and you sense there may be interest in you, ask for it. This isn't the time to let shyness or modesty take over.

After the Interview

9. *Analyze the interview.* Now is a good time to breathe a sigh of relief and think positive thoughts. This is also a good time to objectively analyze your performance. What's your gut feeling? Can you sense there was real interest in you? Were your points made well? Were your questions responded to

and fully answered? Consider each interview an experience. If you realize you made a few mistakes or could have come up with a sharper answer or two, don't dwell on it. Either contact the employer and try to resuscitate your candidacy, or chalk it up as a valuable lesson and concentrate on your next interview.

10. *Follow up.* Following up with a strong thank-you letter is essential to the success of any job search endeavor. Surprisingly, many job seekers overlook this tactful and strategic gesture. In addition to the courtesy and respect it communicates, it keeps your name in front of the hiring authority and reminds your interviewer how well your qualifications fit the position's requirements. What's more, it's an outstanding way to express your sincere interest in the position and the company. Then, if you haven't heard from the employer in two weeks, write a brief script and then call back to ask if you can provide any additional information to help the decision-making process.

If you don't get the job, don't take it personally or get discouraged, even if you thought you were a perfect fit. There could be a dozen reasons why you didn't get the offer, many of which may have nothing to do with you at all. Your focus should be on future interviews—the ones you can still influence—rather than on past meetings you can no longer control.

—Arthur I. Frank, MBA, Resumes "R" Us

TIP #66—TELL YOUR "VALUE" STORIES

One of the most important steps in the job search process is to list the characteristics that make you desirable to a potential employer. For each of the assets that you list, you must illustrate in story form your benefit to the employer. Each of these stories or outstanding contributions in the workplace should include facts and figures to verify your contributions.

The first step in this process is to identify your value to the employer. List as many values as you can. What abilities do you have that would make an employer want to hire you? The following are some sample questions that you may want to consider.

- Can you tackle multiple tasks?
- Are you able to solve difficult and complex problems?
- What specific job skills do you have? What sets you apart from others in your field?
- What specific accomplishments on the job are you particularly proud of?

After completing your value list, go back and rank the potential value of each ability to the employer. You may need to review job announcements for specific skills desired in your career area.

With your value list ranked from most important to least important, think about specific instances that you can describe to illustrate the top 5 to 10 values. Try to find stories that can be documented with percentages and numbers. Almost all employers are in business to make money. How have you helped previous employers meet this objective?

A story follows that might seem insignificant, but in fact became pivotal in one person's job search. A young man worked as a patient relations aide in a large teaching hospital. He noticed that one third of the wheelchairs were unusable. He began a campaign to solve the wheelchair problem. It took him three months, working through appropriate channels in four departments to solve the problem. His supervisor did not respond immediately; however, he did not give up. His ultimate accomplishment—getting the wheelchairs repaired and in usable condition—saved the hospital over $300,000. He demonstrated his ability to successfully tackle a problem (not assigned to him), his finesse in solving it, and his bottom-line financial contributions.

This accomplishment was listed on his resume, noted in an attached letter of recommendation and described by him during job interviews. He started by writing a script describing the situation and his successful resolution. Then he practiced in front of a mirror and with family and friends. When it came time for the actual interview, he was successful in illustrating his problem-solving and communication skills.

The human resource professional with whom he interviewed did not have an actual position for him, but she was so impressed with his potential that she created a position for him with her company, a large hospital in the Los Angeles area. The responsibilities of his new position were to discover problem areas in the medical facility and to propose solutions. He obtained this position because he had identified his potential value to a company, written a story illustrating that value, practiced telling his story, and was able to communicate it effectively in an actual interview.

This example demonstrates just how important it is to have your values identified and then supported with facts and figures. Write a story for each of your top values and then practice that story until you can communicate it flawlessly. When you illustrate your accomplishments (with supporting results), you are speaking the language of the employers. Remember, virtually every company is driven by bottom-line profitability.

—*Lynn Hughes, MA, CPRW, CEIP, A Resume and Career*
Service, Inc.

TIP #67—CAR Strategy for Interview Success

Employers are interested in what you can do for them, not what they can do for you. They want to know how you can make them money, save them money, solve problems, improve the corporate image, and make the company look good. It is your challenge during the interview to respond to and communicate this information.

A proven strategy for accomplishing this is the CAR (Challenge, Action, Results) strategy, a format that allows you to answer the question, "So what?" in reference to your achievements. By using stories of 30 to 40 words for each accomplishment or action, you create a picture in the interviewer's mind by telling what challenge you faced, why it was significant, and how you made a measurable difference. Give specific examples supporting how you used your skills and abilities to bring about these results.

Challenge (What was the problem?): I was recruited to salvage a failing sales and service operation.

Action (What did you do about it?): After assessing the situation, I hired new, talented, educated, and motivated staff, established incentive awards, and instituted quality controls.

Results (What was the measurable result?): Operating expenses dropped 27 percent, sales skyrocketed 68 percent, and customer retention increased 73 percent.

Here's another example:

Challenge: Sales had dropped after two new competitors arrived in the local market.

Action: I set up a structured customer call program to ensure that my staff and I were able to visit all existing accounts personally and make calls to new accounts on a regular basis.

Results: My team and I boosted sales revenues 53 percent and raised our ranking from #9 to #1 in one year for a 30-store auto supply chain.

It is critical that these CAR stories be well rehearsed and well delivered during your interview. As such, take the time to go over them several times with a friend or coach to be sure that you can automatically and powerfully answer the question, "So what?" It will make a huge difference in your presentation in each interview and the impact that you leave behind.

—Nancy Karvonen, CPRW, CCM, JCTC, CEIP,
A Better Word & Resume

TIP #68—PURPOSE OF INTERVIEW #1

The only purpose of interview #1 is an invitation for interview #2. That's it!

With the tremendous complexity of today's job search market, it is extremely rare that you will be offered a position after just one interview. Chances are you will be back interviewing with the company on several occasions before an offer is extended. Don't have any greater expectations. It's a one in a million shot that an offer will be placed on the table that early in the interviewing and hiring process.

Be realistic and know what your job is during interview #1—to impress the interviewer, sell your skills, competitively position yourself against other candidates, and get your name on the short list of prospective candidates returning for the next stage in the company's interview process—interview #2.

—Author's tip

TIP #69—MAKE YOURSELF THREE TIMES MORE LIKELY TO GET HIRED!

Research done by the executive search industry has shown that the first person interviewed gets the job only 17.6 percent of the time. But the last person interviewed is hired 55.8 percent of the time, or more than three times more frequently.

The reason: As in most human endeavors, people are wary of accepting the first choice offered. Therefore, do what you can to position yourself among the last candidates interviewed, and definitely not among the first. Other reasons are corporate inertia . . . it's often customary to move at a glacial pace . . . or the sense of urgency may not exist at the beginning of a search.

Wait 10 days to two weeks before responding to a help-wanted ad. (Aged ads are excellent for this purpose.) If you have a good relationship with your executive recruiter, ask him to wait it out and not propose you too early. And if the interviewer asks you when you can set up an appointment, push the day back as far as possible. Other studies have shown that Monday is the worst day of the week to be interviewed for a job. The worst time for an interview is late afternoon. These are simply guidelines. Merely use them to your advantage whenever possible.

—Arthur I. Frank, MBA, Resumes "R" Us

TIP #70—THE INFORMATION INTERVIEW

As the employment market tightens and finding a new position becomes extra challenging, it is more important than ever to take a proactive approach to job search and lifelong career management. One of the ways you can accomplish this is through the information interview.

Eighty-five percent of all job openings are never advertised, and one of the quickest ways to find a new position is to never ask for one. That's right—*never ask for one!* When you ask somebody for a job you are almost always asking to be turned down. While no one likes to be told there is no position available, another aspect is at work as well. Most people love to help someone in need, but when they are asked for something they cannot give, they feel uncomfortable. And, the more uncomfortable they feel, the quicker they will want to forget you, which is the opposite of what you want to happen.

Honesty is the cornerstone of the job search. You are not trying to hide the fact that you are looking for a job, you are only being reasonable when you assume that a person will not have a job for you or know someone else who does. However, when you make it clear you don't expect them to have an opening, or know of one, the pressure is off, and they will be willing to listen to you and will usually try to help you.

The information interview is perhaps the single most important tool in your job search, and yet it is the area most people ignore. Here's how it works. Call a company and tell them you are exploring opportunities with numerous firms in the area and would like to get some information. Ask for 10 to 15 minutes (in person) to discuss the operations, successes, and long-range goals of the company. You are in charge, you instigate the interview, and you set the agenda. This type of interview puts you in contact with a great number of individuals, increases your chances of finding just the right job, and can be quite enjoyable because you are under no stress to ask for a job. You are simply searching for information and contacts. People love to know you consider them experts in their field and are usually glad to help in any way they can.

There are six steps, or objectives, to each information interview:

1. *Establish rapport.* Have the person identify and feel comfortable with you.
2. *Educate the person.* Show your value by sharing your skills and accomplishments, making sure they understand your major strengths and how you can effectively contribute to the bottom line. The more you share your accomplishments, the easier you make it for others to help you.
3. *Get advice.* Advice genuinely asked for is usually freely given. Ask how they view your skills and if the career you are seeking is appropriate.

4. *Get information.* This is the main reason for the interview. Listen for the latest developments, who is doing what, articles and publications you should read, professional societies you should join, and so on. Absorb all they tell you—write it down and ask questions.

5. *Get referrals.* Say "Can you refer me to other successful individuals like yourself whose advice and guidance would be beneficial?" Not many people will turn down a request like that.

6. *Be remembered favorably.* If you have accomplished the above five steps, you will have no trouble being remembered favorably, but, just to be sure, send a note to each person you interview, thanking them for their time and information. Also, let them know you will keep them informed of your progress. Then, be sure to add them immediately to your database of network contacts.

Your Assignment: Schedule Information Interviews

Go out and do two information interviews this week. There is no other way than simply forcing yourself to do it. Make a list of potential interviewees, pick two, and just do it! You may feel uncomfortable, but it is one of the most effective ways to find the best job for you. What's more, it will give you great practice for when you're interviewing for that all-important "real" job.

The information interview is not only the cheapest, but also the most effective way of getting information on 80 percent of jobs that are never advertised. And, it is the most fun. Invariably, when scheduling an appointment you will say, "Can I have 20 minutes of your time?" and an hour later you will be leaving. It is simply a fact that if someone likes you and understands where you are going, they will want to help you get there.

—*Joyce Fortier, MBA, CCM, CPRW, JCTC, Create Your Career*

TIP #71—LISTEN WELL

Research indicates that almost two-thirds of the time the best qualified candidates don't get the offer and the person chosen often meets fewer than 50 percent of the job qualifications. How can this be?

The reason is because job offers are given most frequently to those candidates who, regardless of formal qualifications, promote themselves best, intimidate least, and listen the most. Strong listening skills allow the candidate to determine or uncover just what the interviewer is looking for. Once this is learned, you have found a perfect way to maximize your opportunity to sell what your potential employer is buying. When you have this vital piece of intelligence, you have everything you need to make a masterful presentation.

A by-product of this is likability. After qualifications, the most important reason an employer will advance your candidacy is because she likes you. And the easiest way to get other people to like you at the start of your relationship is to listen to them attentively.

—Arthur I. Frank, MBA, Resumes "R" Us

TIP #72—DRESS FOR SUCCESS

The old adage is still true—first impressions make lasting impressions and you never get a second chance to make that first impression a good one. Whether you're interviewing for a CEO position or an entry-level bookkeeping position, the style in which you dress instantly communicates a message to a prospective employer. A well-dressed applicant, confident in his/her appearance, makes a tremendously positive impression. Just as your resume is a reflection of your level of competence, employers will perceive your level of professionalism based on your physical appearance. That does not mean you must arrive in a Brooks Brothers' suit. However, if you demonstrate that you care about your appearance, it communicates that you care about your life, your work, and the particular opportunity at hand.

Acceptable standards of professional dress vary greatly by profession, corporate culture, and even geographic region. The old "dress for success" guidelines, such as a three-piece suit and power tie for men and a skirt suit with sensible pumps for women, are no longer accurate for today's diverse corporate cultures. A humorous example of the clash between culture and dress is demonstrated in the movie *My Cousin Vinnie.* When the hero and heroine arrive in a small southern town, their attempts to "blend" with the locals are thwarted by their appearance which screams of their northern origin.

Use the following "dress for success" recommendations when interviewing with prospective employers and when meeting with recruiters, attending job search clubs or networking functions, and interviewing for internal promotions.

When preparing to dress for a job interview, consider the company's corporate culture. Does the organization value tradition and conservatism, creativity and originality, or relationships and reliability? One would dress quite differently if interviewing with a conservative accounting firm versus a start-up advertising agency. In many cases, you will already be familiar with the company's acceptable standard of professional attire. If not, try to observe employees entering and exiting the office in the morning or around lunchtime. Look for a consistency in style you can emulate.

Another suggestion is to dress as your prospective boss might for a meeting with his/her boss or how you might dress to call on the company's biggest client. In addition to interviewing with your prospective boss, you may be required to meet with individuals you would be working directly with (especially if it is a team-oriented company culture), department heads, and persons you would be supervising. As this process may take more than one day, it is advisable to prepare at least three interview outfits.

What if you can't afford a new professional wardrobe? How about borrowing a few pieces from family or friends? If that won't work, try consignment stores. They are a great place to find deals on excellent quality clothing that is "gently used." However, a bargain is only a good deal if the clothes fit well, are in good condition, and are still in relatively up-to-date styles and colors. Other sources of professional clothing might include your local Goodwill store or community charities. The national organization, Dress for Success, offers free business suits to women in need. You can learn more about this organization by visiting *www.dressforsuccess.org.* Once you get the job and are doing well, you might even consider contributing to your community by recycling your own professional wardrobe. The following are a few basics to consider when preparing your interview wardrobe. Because company standards for professional dress vary so greatly, there are no hard and fast rules in dressing for success these days. Therefore, the suggestions below are for general purposes.

Colors and Patterns

Gray, navy, and black are still the safest colors. Wearing bolder colors such as red and royal blue can exude confidence for women, although it is advisable that the style be kept relatively conservative. People in certain professions such as sales and marketing can often wear bolder colors and patterns. Depending on the current styles, stripes and geometric-shaped patterns may be suitable. Polka dots, floral designs, and animal prints are usually viewed more as casual patterns and should be avoided.

Styles

Others may also perceive your ability to maintain awareness of, and flexibility to, changing times based on your style of dress. Do you wear current styles or are you stuck in a past era? Although you don't need to be wearing the trendiest styles (nor is it advisable in most cases), you don't want to age yourself by bringing out and dusting off that three-piece double-knit polyester suit either. If you are unsure about the current trends in colors, patterns, and styles, check out the displays in your local department stores. Give attention to lengths, collar and tie widths, jacket styles, patterns, colors, and accessories. Classic styles of clothing are always a safe bet and can easily be updated by changing accessories.

What do you do if your interview is scheduled on casual Friday? If the organization participates in a casual Friday, it is still advisable to dress as if it were any other workday. Casual Friday is an employee benefit and you are not, as yet, an employee.

Quality

Fabrics such as lightweight wool, natural fibers, wool blends, and other blends are best. Men's ties should be made of 100 percent silk. Leather or an undetectable faux leather substitute is best for shoes, belts, and purses or carrying cases. Well-tailored, well-fitting garments communicate an impeccable style and a distinct professional attitude.

Accessories

When choosing accessories to complete your professional attire, it is safest to abide by the "less is more" philosophy. First, consider the company's standards. For example, one company may consider it unprofessional for a man to wear an earring but another company may consider it a nonissue. Jewelry for women should not be distracting to the interviewer. You want the interviewer focusing on what you are saying and not watching your large dangle earrings move and jingle when you talk. All accessories should be color- and style-coordinated and in good condition. And, don't forget to check your shoes, socks or hosiery, belts, undergarments, eyewear, portfolio cases, handbags, and overcoats.

Personal Grooming

Hair should be clean, in an up-to-date style, and one in which you will not have to fuss with during the interview (e.g., sweeping it out of your eyes). Men with facial hair should be certain it is neatly trimmed and that the company does not frown on beards and mustaches. For women, make-up should be moderate (nothing can be more embarrassing than leaving an interview feeling confident until you discover your teeth are wearing your lipstick too!). Teeth must be flossed and clean, and if it is a breakfast or luncheon meeting, don't forget to find an opportunity to check your teeth, and if possible brush, after eating. Shoes should be shined and clothing pressed.

Be Sure to Bring . . .

What should you take to the interview? Bring several nicely printed copies of your resume and reference pages (references should not be given until you are asked for them), your career portfolio (if appropriate for you/your profession), and questions to ask the interviewer(s). Be sure to bring the names and titles of those you are meeting with, telephone numbers, scheduled appointment times, and driving instructions. Gather business cards and other company information given to you. Have paper and pen available for taking notes. Carry all these items in a hard-cover (preferably leather) portfolio or presentation folder.

It is important to know, whether you are interviewing or are on-the-job, *and* whether accurate or not, that others may presume that your appearance is a direct indicator of the quality of work you produce, your attention to detail, and your level of competency. If the job matters, it matters what you wear!

—*Karen Wrigley, CPRW, JCTC, AMW Career &*
Resume Services

TIP #73—VIDEOTAPE YOUR PERFORMANCE

When you've got a big presentation coming up, what do you do? You practice. What about a marathon you're running in two weeks? You practice. What about a oral examination for an upcoming certification? You practice.

Well, interviewing is no different. In fact, it can be one of the most important presentations of your life. In turn, you need to devote the time and energy to numerous practice sessions so that when you're in the actual interview, your performance is at its peak.

One of the best strategies for interview practice is to videotape your performance. Then you can see, firsthand, what an employer sees—how well you communicate, your body language and posture, how many times you said "Uh" (*not* a good practice!), and how well you listen. Ask a friend, colleague, or your career coach to practice with you. Give them a list of questions you anticipate you may be asked and have them use those during your practice sessions.

Then, take it one step further. Not only do you want to critique your own performance, you want your interviewer to give you feedback—from the actual session and from the videotape. Be sure to take notes about her comments and then work to integrate the ideas into your interview.

Strengthening your performance during an interview goes a long way in positioning yourself above other candidates. Interviewers are skilled at recognizing when a candidate has taken the time to prepare and will be impressed. If you invest just a few hours of your time, you will see immediate results.

—*Diana Bradford, CPRW, JCTC, CareerBound*

TIP #74—PRODUCING YOUR CAREER HIGHLIGHT FILM

What's your favorite spectator sport? Who's your favorite player? How many hours have you spent watching and rewatching his highlight films? What about your film . . . the one that depicts the highlights of your career?

Take a look back over your career and recall the wins, successes, joyous moments, promotions, contributions to teams, clients, organizations, and more. Recall and picture, in vivid detail, the times in your career when you were unstoppable. Then, create a career highlight film that you can conjure up in your head instantaneously and use as the foundation for your 90-second commercial—the one that you'll use over and over in your job interviews when asked, "Tell me about yourself."

This all-important question should not be responded to with a recitation of your life's history—where you were born and grew up, where you went to college, how many kids you have, and the like. Instead, you want to answer this question by sharing the information about you and your career that makes you a superstar—what challenges you've met, what you've achieved, the financial impact of your contributions, and more. Always keep in mind that you want the interviewer to be able to "see" your career highlight film just as you see it. To accomplish that, you must present it with strong, powerful, action-oriented language that conjures up the image of success that you are trying to communicate.

—*Kathy J. Black, MBA, JCTC, Career Recipes*

TIP #75—ASK FOR THE JOB!

That's right—look the interviewer squarely in the eye and ask for the job. Don't pussyfoot around by saying things like "I'm very interested in this position." Say, "May I have the job, please?"

Sound a little strong? Well, don't be afraid of it. Asking for the job can be the best question you'll ever ask.

There's a great deal of misunderstanding about the interview process. Most think it's an event where the company finds out about the candidate's qualifications, and the candidate finds out about the pay, benefits, and career path. On the surface, that seems to be the case. But in actuality, for the company, it's an exercise in Procurement, and for the candidate, it's Sales 101.

Many people don't like the idea that it's sales. Many feel that "their industry is different," that you'd "blow the whole interview" by asking for the job. But, in truth, the interview is a selling situation and the rules of sales apply. It is a foolish salesperson, indeed, who makes the cold call (sends resume), arrives at the appointment, determines the client's needs, makes an effective product demonstration (interview), and then forgets to ask the client if they want to do business (asks for the job).

The key to asking for the job is doing an effective needs assessment. There's an old adage in sales that you can't start selling until the prospect tells you what he's buying. There's a lot of truth to that statement. The problem is that most people approaching an interview misunderstand what a needs assessment truly is—and it's not your skills and qualifications versus the job description.

Needs assessment is where you find out what the company is really trying to hire and why, despite the job description and qualifications statement. If you're a smart candidate, you'll ask questions about behavioral temperaments, where the company sees its future, how the job in question contributes to that future, what kind of leadership is available or needed, and many other questions. During the needs assessment the smart salesperson will also ask questions that force the interviewer to say positive things about the position, the company, and the future. Ask questions like "Where is my manager strong? What does this company or team do well? What is the best thing you can say about this company?" Don't ask about negatives or weaknesses because they don't count. You're the answer to those.

For those of you who've never sold, let me say this: It is imperative that you stay with the "Where are you good?" questioning strategy for as long as possible. Force the interviewer to commend his company at every possible turn. Stick to that message and don't say a word about yourself . . . yet. Why? Because every time the interviewer commends his company, you're going to note that commendation as one of the personal skills and traits you're going to tell them about.

There's a secondary reason to stay on the "Where are you good?" theme. By doing so you associate yourself with excellence, and in turn, that creates a memorable image of you. It's often been noted that either the first or last person in an interview is the one most often hired. If you're stuck in the middle, this positive line of questioning will create a lasting positive image that will help you break out of the pack.

Be prepared to close the interview and ask for the business based on your assessment of the company's needs. Take possession of all those positive things you've discovered about the company and the position, and then describe yourself in those very same terms. Say things such as "I'm very glad to hear that your company excels in customer satisfaction and has one of the best reputations in the nation. In all my experiences, I've made the same type of contributions to my employers and team members."

Once you've gone through every positive point in their needs and your capabilities, summarize and close: "As you can see, I've got the qualifications and temperament to really succeed in this position. May I have the job, please?"

Don't forget the *please* for it's one of the most powerful words in the language. *Please* is the word of extreme sincerity. Remember it from childhood? "Mommy, pleeeeease."

Throughout our lives, we are conditioned by that word and, while most of us haven't used it since grammar school, it hasn't lost its power. Don't dwell on the word and don't emphasize it, but don't leave it out. Most people, even decision makers, hate to say no and asking for the job with a nice *please* added to it makes the "no" response just that much more difficult.

Expect resistance and be prepared to back off. But, also be prepared to push forward as much as possible. As an example, you may get a negative answer because there are other candidates to interview. If so, immediately try to isolate the objection with language such as "I understand that you may not be able to make a decision because you have more candidates to interview, but other than that, do you see anything in my experience that would disqualify me?" If the answer is no, then move toward a conditional close such, as "Well, if there are no problems with my credentials, may I assume that I have the job unless a better candidate arrives?" This question automatically removes all previous candidates from consideration. Human nature is to take the easy road and if you have a conditional close on the interviewer, don't be surprised that the remaining interviews are somewhat perfunctory and you get the job.

—William Murdock, CPRW, The Employment Coach

TIP #76—WRITE POWERFUL THANK-YOU LETTERS

Writing a thank-you letter after an interview is a must; it is appropriate job search etiquette. Employers and recruiters expect it. However, the traditional "Thanks for the interview. . . . Give me the job" letter does nothing to move your candidacy further ahead. Your challenge is to give yourself a significant advantage over your competition, and one way to accomplish that is with a powerful thank-you letter—a letter that says "Thanks for the interview. . . . This is why I'm so great and why I meet or exceed your qualifications. . . . Now, give me the job."

Use your thank-you letters as marketing communications to further sell yourself into your next position. After an interview, you should have much greater insight into what a company needs and expects. Use that information—powerful intelligence—as the foundation for all of your thank-you letters. For example, if developing new technology is the company's #1 goal, stress your experience in technology R&D. If the company is in a turnaround situation, highlight your contributions in other turnarounds and profit-building enterprises. If their focus is on improving sales at the retail store level, highlight your achievements in revenue growth and market expansion. Connect yourself to the company and its needs by clearly documenting the experience you have as it directly relates to their needs.

What's more, you can also use your thank-you letters to overcome objections, should there be any. Suppose the company was looking for an individual with sales experience in the Detroit metro region. However, you've never lived or worked in Detroit. But, you do have many professional contacts in the area. Be sure that information is the focal point of your thank-you letter to virtually eliminate that objection from consideration. What if the company wanted an individual with hands-on experience working with Microsoft Access and, unfortunately, you've never used it before? Mention in your letter that you're proficient with ACT (another database management system) and that you've already proven yourself a quick study of new technologies, so getting a handle on Access shouldn't take any time at all. Let them know you heard their objections and that they are nothing to be concerned about.

You can give yourself a tremendously competitive advantage over other candidates vying for the same position by always remembering the reason you are writing a thank-you letter. It's not really to say "thank you"; it's to again communicate that you're the *right person for the job*!

—*Author's tip*

TIP #77—TRUST YOUR INSTINCTS

You've interviewed three times for a position as logistics manager and finally gotten the offer. The money is good, the commute is only 10 minutes from your house, and you have several colleagues who've worked there in the past. However, something just doesn't feel right and you can't put your finger on it. Is it the company, the position, the corporate culture, or something else? Who knows?

If you find yourself in this position, learn to trust your instincts. If your gut tells you that this is *not* the right opportunity, then turn it down. It's okay to say no. Remember, not only does the employer have to be excited about you, you must be excited about the company and the opportunity. If your sixth sense is telling you that something is amiss, kindly decline the offer and continue looking elsewhere. This is your career and your life!

—Author's tip

Use the "Interview" checklist on pages 167–168 to manage your entire interviewing process effectively.

INTERVIEW CHECKLIST

Directions: Use the following checklist as a step-by-step tool for before, during, and after your interviews.

Before Your Interview

- I have researched the company I am interviewing with. ☐
- I have reviewed my resume so that I can easily address any point brought up during my interview. ☐
- I printed 5 to 10 additional copies of my resume to take to the interview. ☐
- I have practiced my interview performance on numerous occasions. ☐
- I have prepared a list of specific questions to ask at the interview. ☐
- I have determined my key selling points to communicate during the interview. ☐

The Day of the Interview

- I am dressed in a professional manner appropriate for the company and its culture. ☐
- I double-checked to be sure that I had my resumes, letters of reference, notepad, and pen. ☐
- I double-checked my directions to the interview location. ☐
- I have planned my travel to the interview to ensure I arrive 10 minutes before my scheduled interview time. ☐

During the Interview

- I allowed the interviewer to set the pace and tone of the interview. ☐
- I listened intently to all the interviewer had to say and then used that information as the baseline for information that I wanted to communicate about myself and my career. ☐

- I was sure to communicate the key points I had outlined in advance. ☐
- I was sure to highlight my achievements as they related to the position and company. ☐
- I asked what the next step in the hiring process is. ☐
- I asked for the job. ☐

After Your Interview

- I immediately wrote and sent a thank-you note to everyone I interviewed with. ☐
- I evaluated my interview performance and noted both my strengths and weaknesses. ☐
- I marked my calendar to follow up on the appropriate date. ☐
- If one of my network contacts was responsible for facilitating the interview, I immediately forwarded a thank-you note to them to keep them apprised of my situation. ☐

CHAPTER 7

Negotiating Your Best Salary and Compensation Package

TIP #78—WORKING YOUR WAY THROUGH THE MONEY MAZE

Negotiating your salary and compensation package can be tricky! You certainly do not want to price yourself out of the market, nor do you want to settle for less than what you are worth. It's almost always a difficult situation. Here are a few strategies that can help.

If a prospective employer asks you for your salary requirements, use one of the following four responses:

1. Are you making me an offer? (This one's the best!)
2. What is the salary range you had in mind?
3. What was the previous person in this position paid?
4. What does the company believe this job is worth?

Better than 75 percent of the time, your interviewer will respond with some basic information about what the company is offering or planning to pay. This gives you the baseline you need in order to start negotiating to your advantage. And, you do always want to negotiate and ask for more. If you don't try, you won't ever know if you could have negotiated an increase in the initial salary offering from $35,000 to $38,000 or from $225,000 to $275,000. First offers are not usually final offers; your interviewer expects you to negotiate.

If, however, you ask one of those four questions and the interviewer does not provide any information, it all falls back into your lap. Then you might try one of the following five responses:

1. If you could just give me a general ballpark figure of what the company has in mind, it would give me a good place to start in our negotiations. (Try again to get them to throw out a number.)

2. I've researched what other companies pay for positions of this nature and according to that research, I believe my value is worth $75,000 per year to your company. (Allows you to ask for whatever is appropriate for the position, regardless of what your past salary was.)

3. My current salary is $50,000 per year. In order for me to make a move, I need at least a 15 percent annual increase. (Ideal if you're currently employed.)

4. My most recent salary was $100,000 per year. As such, I'm currently anticipating at least $150,000 for a position at this level of responsibility. (Good strategy if you're looking for a significant promotion or leap in level of responsibility.)

5. I prefer to delay our salary conversation until I have met with the other company executives and can better determine if we're a good match. (Another strategy for delaying the inevitable.)

—Author's tip

TIP #79—NEGOTIATE NOW!

People think a recession is the worst time to ask for more money. But I know that it can be the best! If you understand why, you can take advantage of the situation and put money in the bank. Here's a great negotiating tip:

In good times money flows freely, and it's hard to find good people because unemployment is low. So companies staff up with marginal people who can do the job, but they're not really excited about them. When times get tough again, employers start to trim their staffs and the first people they let go are those marginal performers. Then they're really in trouble! They still have to get the work done with not enough staff to do it. Because of layoffs they now have three or four salaries available to hire one or two people. So they're desperately looking for good people, now, not marginal ones, and they have the money to pay them.

If you're one of the "survivors," and have taken over extra responsibilities, ask for a raise. If you're interviewing from the outside, stand your ground and negotiate for ample compensation. They need you more than ever.

And, if cash flow is tight in the company, use another hard-times tactic: ask for more money in clever ways that don't require a cash outlay by the employer. Here are two proven strategies:

1. Ask for more money in terms of time. The average numbers of hours worked per week has risen steadily over the past 20 years. Personal time has become a tremendously valuable commodity. If you can't get a cash raise, why not ask for more vacation or Friday afternoons off? Think about it: noon to 5:30 p.m. off on Fridays adds up to almost seven weeks of vacation! If you arrange it all correctly, you can still do the work you need to do and take the time off, too.

I worked with a client who was putting in 10 to 14-hour days on the job. It was stressful, but he felt he needed to be there to do the ongoing problem solving. Since he was putting in those days already, I coached him to go to his supervisor and propose a four-day week of 10 hours per day (knowing he'd put in 11 to 12 hours a day anyway). They agreed! So he was able to take something he was doing already (long days) and negotiate time off he never would have had otherwise.

There are plenty of other ways to negotiate time. There's flextime, personal days, and payment for unused vacation time. You can also negotiate for "comp time" for days you spend at conventions, trade shows, late with customers, and more. By paying attention and asking for more time, you can significantly increase your income dollars per hour and reclaim some of your lost personal time.

2. Try a little gambling on the job. Now, don't panic! I'm not advocating running a poker game in the cafeteria; I mean betting your boss that you will meet or exceed a target. Construction deadlines, production deadlines, sales quotas, customer satisfaction survey results, cleanliness awards, employee productivity measures, and accident-free days—these are just a few of the targets bosses will reward you for.

Suggest to your boss that reaching a certain goal be rewarded not only with a pat on the back, but a few (thousand) dollars in your paycheck as a bonus. Prove yourself an asset—in good times and bad—and your boss will be happy to compensate you, in traditional or nontraditional ways.

—*Jack Chapman, Lucrative Careers, Inc.*

TIP #80—Saying Nothing Says a Lot

Picture this. You've interviewed three times with a well-established insurance company. You're really interested in the position and, what's more important, they're really interested in you. The only problem you're facing is a salary offer which is less than you anticipated. Do you just walk away? *No!* Try this:

Take a sheet of notebook paper and on the top of the left-hand side of the page, write *Pros*. Then list all the great things about the position. It should be a lengthy list that fills that whole side of the page and includes information about how wonderful everything is—the company, the people, the technology, the products, the potential, and much more.

Then, on the top right-hand side of the page, write *Cons*. In the list, simply write "low salary." That's it.

During your next interview, share this piece of paper with the hiring decision maker at an appropriate time. Tell him that you're so excited about the position that you wrote down all of the great things about the opportunity. Never even mention salary.

Are you showing this piece of paper so that your interviewer will see all the Pros? *No!* However, the interviewer will certainly be impressed that someone of your caliber, someone they're interested in hiring, thinks so highly of the organization.

What you're really doing, however, is showing the interviewer the one thing that could blow the deal for them—your salary. Often this little trick is all that needs to be done. Wait a few minutes, hours, or days, and you may be delightfully surprised with a much higher offer than was originally placed on the table.

—Author's tip

TIP #81—ALTERNATIVES TO INSTANT CASH

When you're negotiating your compensation package, consider things other than simply base salary. Openness and flexibility in proposing and considering a variety of options can benefit you in several ways.

First, it can help both you and the employer from coming to an impasse over a fixed salary figure. Second, other means of compensation might yield greater rewards. Third, depending on tax consequences, an alternative to cash might deliver far greater "real" value than its monetary worth. And finally, you can negotiate hardest for the things that are most important to you.

Here are several compensation and benefits options worth considering:

- *Bonus based on predetermined, very specific performance measurements for you or your team.* For instance, if you're a call center manager, you might negotiate a specific sum or percentage of your salary for each percentage-point improvement in your company's customer satisfaction rating or for every 10-second reduction in average call-response time.

- *Bonus or raise based on tenure.* If the company is reluctant to raise its salary offer due to its current cash situation or because of other timing issues, you might negotiate for a bonus or salary increase after three months, six months, nine months, or one year, as long as you're meeting performance standards.

- *Commission based on measurable increases in profit, revenue, or cost savings you're able to achieve for an initiative you'll be leading.* This reduces the company's risk in hiring you and gives you tremendous motivation to deliver the best possible results for the company (and gain direct benefit from your effort).

- *Stock options offered both as a reward for performance and as a retention strategy for valued employees.* Often reserved for senior managers and executives, at some companies stock options have made millionaires among rank-and-file employees as well. Of course, there is no guarantee that a stock option will be worth a dime when it's exercised. But if you believe in the long-term growth of the company, you may be smart to choose future options over present dollars.

- *Promotion within a specified period of time.* If you're coming into a job at a lower level than you're qualified for—or if you are determined to fast-track your career—a guaranteed promotion with a commensurate salary raise may be worth negotiating before you accept an offer. Of course, the company will want to build in performance criteria to protect themselves.

- *"Golden parachute" or other exit compensation.* The more narrow your niche and the more daunting the challenges that face you, the more you'll want to consider having an advantageous exit agreement in place before you accept an offer.

- *Extra vacation.* Moving to a new company might take your earned vacation time from four weeks to one, depending on company policies. An extra week or two of personal time might be worth more to you than even a comparable cash benefit.

- *Education and professional development.* Will the company pay for your MBA? Will they sponsor you for professional development programs? Unless this benefit is clearly defined in company-wide policy, be sure to have it spelled out in your hiring agreement.

- *Company car, health club membership, professional association dues, box seats at sporting or theater events.* When negotiating, ask about company sponsorship of items that you would otherwise pay for out of your own pocket.

- *Flextime, time off for volunteer projects, freedom to attend your child's ballet recital or soccer game.* What is the company's formal policy in these areas? How willing are they to bend the policy? How important are these issues to you?

- *Medical and insurance benefits.* If you're considering two comparable offers, give each company's health and insurance benefits package a very close look. A more comprehensive package, a lower copay fee or deductible, a high-dollar life-insurance policy—savings to you from these programs can be substantial.

Before starting to negotiate, have a clear picture of your ideal compensation and benefits package. Then, make it your negotiating strategy to win concessions in the areas that are most important to you while giving in on less-important items. Remember, you know what it takes to keep you motivated and productive, so you're really negotiating a win-win outcome for both you and your new employer.

—*Louise Kursmark, CPRW, JCTC, CEIP, CCM,*
Best Impression Career Services, Inc.

TIP #82—ARE THOSE TOLEDO DOLLARS OR NEW YORK CITY DOLLARS?

Do you think that the cost of living in San Francisco is more or less than in Greensburg, Pennsylvania? What about Chicago compared to Eureka Springs, Arkansas? Or Dallas compared to Clemson, South Carolina?

Geography can dramatically impact the dollars you will be paid and that's okay. The reality is that a $50,000 salary in San Francisco would leave you almost destitute while that same salary in Greensburg would allow you to live quite nicely!

The point is that you should not be hasty in turning down an offer in a city that you don't know just because you think the salary is too low. Do your research to learn about the cost of living in that area. How much does an average house cost? Are private schools affordable? What is the annual tax burden? What about auto insurance costs? These are all important considerations you must weigh when evaluating each and every opportunity. It's not about salary . . . it's about how that salary will be spent and how far it will go.

—*Author's tip*

TIP #83—TALK TO AN ATTORNEY

With increasing frequency, companies ask employees to sign employment contracts, consulting contracts, noncompete agreements, confidentiality agreements, and a host of other hiring-related documents.

Be forewarned! Unless it is a document with which you are familiar or it is so easy to read that your 5-year-old child would get it, have it reviewed by an attorney before you sign on the dotted line. The minor investment in legal fees is definitely worth it—for your piece of mind and to prevent any potential misunderstandings between you and your new employer. Don't make the mistakes that others have made and lived to regret!

—Author's tip

TIP #84—REMIND YOURSELF IT'S *NOT* JUST ABOUT MONEY

If you're reading this book, chances are you're just like the rest of us, working to make a living, pay your mortgage, feed and clothe your children, and enjoy an occasional vacation. You don't have a trust fund, you're not going to win the lotto, and your estranged multi-million-dollar uncle is never going to appear!

However, remind yourself that your career is not just about money. It's also about self-worth, pride, and a feeling of contribution. It's about your quality of life, the quality of your personal and professional relationships, and the success you feel within. It's about your personal and professional growth, new adventures, new opportunities, and more. It's about being happy, a concept many job seekers forget when they're vying for their next job, often feeling the pressure to take it even though they know they're not going to like it (and, most likely, not stay in the position for a long time).

I'm not diminishing the importance of money by any means. It is vital to sustain our lives in the style and manner in which we choose to live. But, it's *not* all about money. There are so very many other things that contribute to a happy and fulfilled life, and they cannot be overlooked. They are just as critical when evaluating a job offer as is the money. Don't allow yourself to forget that.

—Author's tip

TIP #85—CELEBRATE

You forwarded a resume, successfully managed four tough interviews at the company, and just negotiated the best compensation package of your life! Now, don't forget to give yourself a hearty pat on the back for a job well done. Don't let yourself get so lost in the process of job search that you forget to reward yourself when the job is complete! You have accomplished what others are constantly striving for— a great new job. You deserve the recognition, so enjoy it.

Then, take it one step further and let everyone else know. You'll most likely send personal notes to family, friends, and colleagues who've been part of your support network or helped with your search. Next, you'll notify your entire network of contacts, thanking them for their assistance, letting them know about your new position and new responsibilities, and reminding them that you're always interested in new opportunities that may arise (not that you're actively job searching).

The next step is to get the word out to the professional community, and the most efficient method for doing this is through the use of a press release. Often, the hiring company will do this for you as you come aboard. If not, then write a press release announcing your new position and send it to local and regional newspapers, radio and television stations, professional associations, and more. Be sure to send a small black and white photograph of yourself along with your press release. Statistics have repeatedly shown that press releases are more likely to get published if they are accompanied by a photo.

Not only does it feel great to get publicity, you are also actively building your name recognition, your brand, and your network. All of these are extremely important concepts, as you've read earlier in this book, and are essential to your success in lifelong career management.

—Author's tip

CHAPTER 8

Lifelong Career Management for Professional Success

TIP #86—Job Security Comes from Within

After 30 years of dedicated service to a job that he could count on every day, Ray Davis of Kansas City retired in 1981 with a good pension from a large major airline. He was set for life and could now spend his time with family and friends, travel, read, and enjoy a host of recreational activities he never had time for when he was working.

In striking contrast, the job scene differs today. William Smith of Kansas City, a retail store manager, was laid off after 38 years with a national home improvement chain. Instead of severance benefits, Mr. Smith received a claim form to file with the bankruptcy court as his company shut its doors and forced thousands out of work.

Unfortunately, many of us will not see rewards from our employers for the years we put into our careers. In fact, most of us won't spend our entire lives working for only one employer. The long-held

American dream of retiring from one company after a lifetime of service is no longer a realistic expectation for today's workforce. Instead, thousands of workers who believed in a traditional employment covenant have already fallen victim to company downsizings, right-sizings, reorganizations, mergers, and other such internal changes. And more layoffs will certainly follow as companies struggle to survive in a recession-plagued economy.

How can we sustain our careers in a work world where there is no job security? Simply put, today's job security must come from within ourselves. We must ensure our own job security by becoming so competent and so self-confident in whatever we do that we can do it anywhere. We accomplish this by adopting an assertive learning style, earning that college degree, or completing that advanced training. We do it by attending professional seminars and networking with colleagues. We do it by becoming experts in our fields, sharing our knowledge, and proving to others that we have what it takes to do it best. We ask our companies for cross training and we volunteer our services for special projects. We proactively search for ways to update our skills, knowing that change is the only constant in the workplace. Acknowledging that no employee is indispensable, we don't take our jobs for granted. Instead, we accept that every day we must continue to earn the right to keep our positions.

By taking calculated risks, you can build job security. Submit that application for a new and challenging position, even if you are comfortable and satisfied with your present job. Always be ready for the unexpected. Don't wait until the proverbial handwriting appears on your company wall. Take charge of your own career so that you can design your own happy, productive life and future.

Adopt a "heads-up" approach to career transition to enhance your job security. This begins with updating your resume as soon as you start a new job. That way you always have a current resume ready to submit on a moment's notice. Have you ever seen that perfect position in the help-wanted ads, but didn't have time to write a resume prior to the application deadline? The worst time to write your resume is when you are hit with an unexpected termination or layoff. When this happens, emotions take their toll and make it next to impossible to organize your thoughts into a sharp, interview-getting resume.

If you are concerned about your job security, seek career coaching to help you focus on what you want in your career. What is your life purpose? Define your career values and determine your motivated skills with the support of a qualified career coach. Evaluate your career interests to construct the right career action plan for you. Ask a career coach to help you prepare for job interviews and work with you on a multilevel job search campaign.

Make friends with the unknown by embracing change as an opportunity for career growth and continued job security. "Fortune favors the bold" is an observation of Virgil, a wise poet of long ago, that holds true even today. Are you bold enough to create your own job security? You will need to do just that to survive in today's rapidly changing world of work. Our economy has witnessed thousands of layoffs since the start of the new millennium; signs point to the potential for many more to come.

—*Meg Montford, CCM, CPRW, Abilities Enhanced*

TIP #87—DEVELOP A SURVIVOR MENTALITY

Never Assume You'll Be Safe

From my years as a corporate human resources professional, I learned that those who survived hard times were inevitably those who felt they would be the next to be laid off. Funny how it works that way. The reason, I think, is fairly simple. If you are always assuming you'll be hit, you'll be more likely to be on the lookout for new opportunities—either within your current company or externally. That way, when changes come, you are prepared to take the next step.

Often, you will see people who, seemingly without effort, land on their feet. What you don't see is the amount of preparation this takes.

For example, a few years ago, a friend of mine saw that budgets were being slashed in her department. She surmised that headcount reductions would be next. Her peers had blinders on and were oblivious to their environment. She, on the other hand, spent every free minute speaking to people in other parts of the company, networking, and learning where the openings were. She landed a new job in another department just in time. Over 50 percent of her former colleagues were laid off.

Who Is Retained?

Well, that's fine, some people will say. But, they never get rid of top performers. First, lose the notion that good people are always valuable and always kept. Companies today need to make certain numbers that require them to make significant reductions in force. The employees can be talented, mediocre, or anywhere in between. When numbers need to be met, everyone goes. This is often a startling shock for many top performers who thought they would always be safe. A shock like this can often cause the person to withdraw, even become bitter in some cases—not a good state of mind to begin a job search.

How Do You Develop a Survivor Mindset?

How do you acquire this skill set if you don't have it? What you need to do first is listen and observe. If you are employed, listen to water cooler gossip. Listen to what the mailroom workers are saying. Learn to read between the lines. For example, if you hear from the person that delivers your mail that they are currently reprogramming all of their equipment with a different address, you may want to ask, what is the new address? Some information can't be shared, but often people are a wealth of knowledge and give it away freely with just one little question. You might begin some research on that new address. Is it larger or smaller than the current company building? If it's smaller, you might surmise that fewer people will be needed. Perhaps layoffs are imminent. Some may say this leads to paranoia. It does, in a way, but a healthy paranoia can help keep you afloat and ahead of the competition.

Design a Plan

After getting a hint that changes will be coming, you need to design a plan of action. Work with "what if" scenarios. For example, if my department is eliminated, where would I look for a new job? Or, if my department were to be merged with another department, what functions would be kept? This doesn't need to be elaborate, but does need to be written. Some elements of your plan might be to update your resume, reconnect with your network, research your industry and other industries that may be thriving, and join a job search support group. Give yourself due dates and stick to them. I recommend that you actually write down the steps of this plan. Nothing helps make things happen better than the written word. If you write it, you internalize it and make it happen!

What Benefits Does It Provide?

The benefits are numerous, but most significantly, developing a plan will give you peace of mind. Just knowing that you are covering all your bases and keeping yourself one step ahead is reassuring. Also, you may be surprised by some wonderful opportunities you uncover that you hadn't realized were there. Even if nothing dire happens, you may launch yourself on a totally new career path that you find much more rewarding. The new path may require some additional training, and what better time to get it than when you are currently employed.

What If the Worst Scenario Happens?

The worst happens and you are laid off. First and foremost, keep your wits about you! If you read the first part of this tip, you will not be off guard. You knew it was coming, but maybe did not know just when. The news may be a shock, but not nearly as shocking as to your coworkers who never saw it coming. But you have a plan that puts you one step ahead of everyone else. You will survive!

—*Fran Kelley, MA, CPRW, SPHR, JCTC, The Resume Works*

TIP #88—ACCUMULATING CAREER RESALE VALUE

Two important things occur when one turns 16 . . . the opportunity to get that first job and the strong desire to get your driver's license. For years we watch others shift the gears, accumulating in-depth knowledge regarding the rules of the road. However, never are we taught about choosing a place to work. We buy road maps for a vacation but never bother to map a route for the three, four, or five decades that we will be earning a living.

To operate an automobile, we are required to complete a formal classroom course followed by a designated amount of hours on the road accompanied by an instructor. Finally, before we ever enter a vehicle and choose a direction, we have to pass a driving test. It is the law, and today we can pretty much assume that everyone on the highway has been trained, tested, and licensed.

Considering the rituals required to simply maneuver a motor vehicle, it is nothing short of amazing that we do not offer, commit, or require this same analysis and preparation in career planning. After all, don't we confront our adorable little ones in the middle of family gatherings with, "What do you want to be when you grow up?" Why does this exercise end with their answers of "cowboy" and "ballerina?" Why, until years later when someone again asks, "What's your major?" is the subject rarely mentioned? And why, even then, is there little or no career planning guidance in one's decision to take a job?

It is long past time to focus on the fact that candidates receive very little training in career planning. For decades, professionals have committed to job offers based on nothing more than the fact that their employers appeared in the help-wanted ads. Unfortunately the results of ill-defined priorities and nonexistent strategies, critical to career planning and advancement in the toughest of job markets, have left many a candidate with no professional identity and thus no direction when forced to make a change.

The best foundational growth strategy to leverage career advancement is clearly defined as "seeking and accepting a job offer based on its ability to score future job offers." It is a foolproof method meant not only to secure employment but also ensure continued career growth in spite of a recessionary climate. It requires discipline, even in prosperity.

Candidates are traditionally defined by the functions they perform and the environments in which they are performed (e.g., controller in a manufacturing setting, director of sales in a consumer products company). If these candidates are good career planners, they change jobs based not necessarily on vertical promotion (e.g., warehouse supervisor to logistics manager, director of finance to CEO), but on securing alternative opportunities, even those that may require some sacrifice in order ultimately to ensure more options.

Savvy career planners can be college students or midlife career changers. They set long-term goals and search for vehicles and paths with several stops to achieve those goals. More important than compensation, location, or status, they know that adding a resale morsel gained from wise planning will someday open doors perhaps closed to others. This resale morsel can be a college degree, a certification, a new product environment, or a job function never before performed.

It is never too early or late to configure your plan. In advance of your job search, make a list of those things critical to increasing your ultimate career resale value. The risk of making the wrong decision based on emotion will be reduced because you have created guidelines for yourself. Know why you are accepting a job offer. Look toward the future and be flexible with the knowledge that your value will continue to increase.

—Janice Worthington, CPRW, JCTC, CEIP,
Worthington Career Services

TIP #89—GOOD THINGS COME TO THOSE WHO VOLUNTEER

Community service is important in its own right, but the rewards reaped from volunteerism at work go way beyond the good feeling you get for your effort and a pat on the back from the boss.

Volunteering at work can make all the difference when your boss is forced to decide which employee is looking at early retirement. When it comes down to you and the guy in the cubicle next door, a history of stepping up to the plate can serve to keep you in the ranks of the employed. Putting forth extra effort and going above and beyond not only marks you as a team player in your boss' eyes, but helps you stand out above the crowd in the eyes of your colleagues, coworkers, and peers in other departments.

Make that extra effort and step up to the plate when a project is falling behind. When you know that the team could use an extra pair of hands, offer to take on the tasks no one else wants or come up with some great ideas for improving the processes already in place. Taking on added responsibilities during times of high production can ensure that your efforts and value to the company won't be forgotten during slowdowns.

Attain star status by taking on a difficult but high-profile task that has been talked about but never implemented. Research what is needed, the steps you can take to make it happen, and set goals and deadlines just like any other project. Achieve the set goals for this project and you will have ensured yourself a gold star in your boss' book of employees.

Volunteer wisely. In addition to making you the star player in your boss' eyes, volunteering for unwanted tasks, on occasion, creates goodwill among colleagues and team members. While you don't want to get stuck with the grunt work on every project, coworkers recognize when someone is honest in their desire and efforts to help. Be cautious in your efforts though; too much volunteering or volunteering only for high-profile assignments can work against you in office politics. Volunteering only for assignments that reap benefits for yourself or not allowing others an opportunity to contribute can create an atmosphere of hostility and resentment among your coworkers, pushing you back down the ladder of success faster than you can climb up.

Lastly, follow through on the commitments you make and don't overcommit. Be sure you have the time and energy to handle added projects and still do a great job in your job!

—Shanna Kemp, M.Ed., IJCTC, CPRW, CCM,
Kemp Career Services

TIP #90—RECESSION-PROOF YOURSELF AND GET A RAISE

There are only two kinds of employers: the one you work for now and the one who will hire you next. Both must have—but rarely get—information they need to hire, retain, and promote the best people. Simply put, those employees who contribute the most to the bottom line will always be in demand, even in the worst recessions. This strategy will help put you in that select group and keep you there. But to understand why this system works so well, an examination of the workplace in tough times is in order.

The economy slows when profits start falling. Companies have only two ways to compensate: boost sales or cut costs. Because people buy less in a sluggish economy, generating more sales may be outside the company's control. However, companies cut costs relatively quickly to stay profitable. The first cuts are often in personnel because that's where a lot of money can be saved fast.

People often think layoffs are done by a formula, such as "last hired, first fired." The reality is more complicated. Because companies must get smaller, each member of the team must be a top producer. Slowdowns, therefore, are a chance to replace the "just OK" employees with "superstars." That approach not only helps firms get through hard times, it positions them well when business picks up again. And it can help you not only ride out a recession, but even move forward.

People rarely grasp the real value of excellence, even though the "80-20" rule applies: 80 percent of the work is done by the top 20 percent of workers. Your supervisor is often too busy solving problems to keep track of your best work. And, you may assume you are "just doing my job." You can't always change a manager's appreciation of your success, but you can certainly be sure you get credit for all you do. No one else will.

It's not the job title you hold, nor the responsibilities listed in your position description that make you recession-proof. It's how much you contributed to your company's bank account. Said another way, it's how you solved the problems that once limited your organization's profitability. After all, no matter what your job title says, you were hired to be a problem solver. And it's up to you to document what you did, how you did it, and what the results were.

Few of us can make an enormous impact on the job. Success usually comes in finding and exploiting opportunities over time. Therefore, your success stories needn't be earth shattering, just illustrative. Think of each of your contributions as a three-step process. You found a problem, you came up with a solution, and you got results. Document the process along those lines every week. How you capture the information isn't important. Keep notes in a word processing file. Jot down some information on a piece of paper. Punch it into your PDA. But do it—and do it every week.

Your stories will be much more powerful if you'll consider these suggestions. First, make the story come alive. You don't have to include proprietary or personal information to make the impact plain. There is even a test to be sure you are on the right track: did I lay out each one of the three steps outlined above? If you haven't, your notes probably only state a responsibility, not an outcome. Second, show the impact. Business runs on numbers, so quantify whenever you can. Then compare your work with previous results or a company standard. Finally, if there is a special context, make it clear: quantify, compare, and place it in context.

Let's look at an example. "After others with more experience tried and failed, I sought out our competitor's best salespeople and convinced some to join our team. Impact: one new salesperson brought 90 percent of her customer base and nearly $50 million in sales—the largest increase we've had in 10 years." The context is certainly there ("After others with more experience had tried"). The payoffs are quantified ("$50 million"). The outcome is compared with earlier results ("the largest increase we've had in 10 years").

You can then use this information to get a raise. About two weeks before your performance report is due, polish those success stories and attach them to a short note to your boss. The note reminds him that your performance review is coming and that you often solve problems without taking his time. You've attached a list of examples in hope that they will be a good baseline to discuss how you can increase your contributions to the company. Yes, you've communicated, without saying it, that you will ask for a raise. But you've also made it easy for your boss to say yes with solid evidence of your worth. If the company sees you as a valuable investment and compensates you for your contributions (e.g., salary increase, bonus, performance incentive), you'll probably want to stay with them. If, however, they don't appreciate your efforts, it's time to use your notes in another way.

The same success stories are the key to a better job. Consider the impact of a resume that has proof of performance. Most resumes that hiring managers see are little more than dry recitations of responsibilities and job titles. Then, they see *your* resume, full of accomplishments and specific examples of your contributions. You've made the decision to interview and hire you easy!

In summary, document what you do before your next review and increase your chances of being retained during a downsizing. Capture those same stories in your resume and you'll be very marketable, no matter what direction the economy takes.

—*Don Orlando, MBA, CPRW, JCTC, CCM,*
The McLean Group

TIP #91—CONTINUE LEARNING

The most effective way to cope with change and find the opportunities it offers is to continue learning. It doesn't matter what your age or place in life is . . . change affects us all. And we are the sum of what we experience, read, hear, and learn. Don't rely only on prior work experiences and past education to help you maintain or move forward in your career.

Since people no longer have one linear career for a lifetime, it becomes critical to recognize the importance of training and education even after "formal education" ends. Whether looking for a new job or career, or becoming more valuable in your current job, continuous learning is imperative. Even people in business for themselves must engage in lifelong learning to remain competitive.

The first step is to open your mind and acknowledge where you are. Take some time to learn about yourself by assessing your motivated skills, values, interests, and personality style. This process will give you a solid basis around which to set your goals and orient your direction and your life. Talents, strengths, and personality are enduring and will allow you to function best in an environment that gives you a chance to show your worth.

Learn what energizes you, keeps you in the flow, gives you a feeling of deep satisfaction, and which you do as naturally as breathing. This will make you sharp and give you focus and clarity so you can reach consistent and near-perfect performance. Anything you learn rapidly is a clue that you're in a strength area. Stop wasting time with energy drainers.

Become informed about trends and themes of emerging business, and stay informed . . . about new ideas, programs, classes, and advances. Seek out diversity, new friends, new ideas, and different thinking styles, and learn from them. Observe and understand how new technologies will impact various industries, small businesses, education, and community life. Explore the Internet, magazines, newspapers, trade journals, and professional organizations for recurring themes that might be useful to you. Develop entrepreneurial thinking and a reputation for problem solving and offering solutions to difficult issues.

Career-resilient and successful people make it a point to learn something new every day . . . to gain ideas from every place they go and everyone they meet. Some action ideas to try:

- Start an idea file, and commit 30 minutes every day to actively seeking new information and an additional 10 minutes to deciding how that information could be applied in your life.

- Be curious and follow your curiosity. Attend professional conferences and meetings. Investigate ideas/trends and explore them until you fully understand and can articulate your opinions clearly to others.

- Jump-start your creativity by taking some quiet time every day to allow new ideas to generate on demand. Use your intuition and subconscious to capture ideas and write them down.

- Actively seek out different stimuli, friends, volunteer opportunities, news media, new challenges, and new ways of communicating and motivating others.

Use all available resources effectively. Learn what the experts in your field are talking about. Stop waiting and take action: read a book, take a course, enroll in a graduate program, volunteer somewhere you would like to learn more about, or learn a new technology.

—*Linsey Levine, MS, JCTC, CareerCounsel*

TIP #92—PREPARE FOR GROWTH

Don't ever assume that just doing your job—even doing it very well—is good enough. To protect your current position and prepare yourself for the future you should constantly be seeking new ways to improve the skills you have and add to your abilities and areas of expertise.

Identify opportunities for growth and improvement by finding out what you will need to know. Search employment ads for positions similar to and just above the one you have now. What skills are employers seeking? Do you have that training and experience? If not, how and where can you get it?

Depending on the type of training and education you need, there are many options. Consider these:

- *Enhance your soft skills such as communications, interpersonal relationship building, organization, time management, and even leadership and management through reputable training companies that offer skill-focused courses.* There are many large training companies that offer seminars nationally on a rotating basis—your HR or training department may have access to that information. If not, a quick search on the Internet for "training" will identify many opportunities.
- *Build your computer skills and knowledge through software-specific training.* Check with local computer stores for PC training available through them or a software manufacturer. You can often train yourself with a little motivation and determination by using online software training.

- *Seek training from within.* If promotion to management with your current company is your goal, learn everything you can regarding company policies and procedures, hiring laws, and the overall corporate structure through company-sponsored training and education. If your company has a training department, chances are they can offer you the education you need on-site.

- *Hire a career coach.* Many successful professionals attribute their career and personal growth to the support and assistance they received from a professional coach. A career coach offers expertise in analyzing your professional abilities as well as your personal desires for the future. A qualified coach will guide you in improving immediate performance as well as in preparing for the future in the best possible way.

- *Advance your formal education.* Never got around to completing your degree? Want to brush up on some newer methods and schools of thought through traditional education venues? Many junior colleges and universities offer courses available to nontraditional students or those not enrolled in a specific degree. Many managers complete their MBAs through weekend-only educational programs that allow them to focus on the job during the week. If time or distance still offers a roadblock to success, consider one of the many reputable online universities that offer degree programs. Many offer monthly start dates, flexible deadlines for completed assignments, and progress-at-your-own-rate programs. Be sure your selection is accredited and check for references from satisfied students.

- *Learn from those who do.* Seek out a mentor who can offer advice and guidance in improving your personal and professional skills. Bosses are often flattered that you find them leadership material and will go out of their way to offer you learning opportunities and information when they know you are serious about advancement. Before you start, be sure you are open to hearing both positive and negative comments on your performance and are ready to make the necessary changes and effort to accomplish your goals.

Finances always come into play when seeking advanced training and education. Contact the HR department at your company and see what your options are for getting tuition and training reimbursement if you take college or computer courses independently. Most companies want their employees to learn and are willing to at least share in the expense. Many offer a tuition reimbursement package based on your performance—the better you do, the more they pay. While this can mean an initial outlay of funds for you, many universities work with students on tuition reimbursement schedules and will delay billing until the end of the semester if you can provide proof of company reimbursement.

Being prepared with the right set of skills—combined with doing your current job very well—will put you ahead of colleagues when promotion time comes around, help protect the position you do have in the event of layoffs, and ensure your successful future.

—Shanna Kemp, M.Ed., IJCTC, CPRW, CCM,
Kemp Career Services

TIP #93—BE VISIBLE

Visibility breeds familiarity and familiarity breeds desire.

If you make yourself visible and become a known entity in your profession and/or your industry, opportunities will come knocking at your door.

Consider these high-profile, visibility-building initiatives:

- Attend local meetings of professional associations in your area (e.g., American Marketing Association, American Society for Quality, Society for Human Resource Management) to meet and greet other professionals in your industry.

- Assume a leadership role in a professional or industry-related association.

- Speak at professional meetings, conferences, workshops, and seminars that are attended by professionals within your targeted industry and/or profession.

- Make media contacts and get quoted in major publications that hiring managers and executives in your industry read.

- Write articles for online or print publication in newspapers, magazines, professional journals, industry-specific websites, and more.

- Write a book on a business-related topic or collaborate with another professional in your field.

- Volunteer within your local community at an organization or not-for-profit agency where other "movers and shakers" are involved.

- Network, network, and network some more. Always stay in touch with your network and keep adding to the list.

—Author's tip

TIP #94—CREATE A SECOND PAYCHECK

"Who's got time for part time?" you may ask. You're already loaded down with a 40-plus hour-a-week job and all the other demands on your time. Well, let me assure you, there are businesses you can start and run in fewer hours per week than Monday night football and a trip to the shopping mall. I'll show you how to find them in the last two paragraphs, but first let's examine why owning your own business can be better than a job.

If you can create the time, there are two big advantages to running your own business: (1) you can never be fired (but you can always quit!) and (2) if you pick it right, you can build profits that are better than wages.

Wages (salaries) exchange dollars for time. Since your time is limited, your dollars are limited too. The only way to make more wages without more time is to negotiate a raise or find a new job, both of which can be difficult. On the other hand, in your own business, you can make more money which is not necessarily tied to more time. Here's an example in real estate; the principles will apply to any career field.

Let's say that you work for a company in the property management industry. If this is the case, the only way to earn more money on that job is to trade more hours of your life working. When hard times hit, you're let go.

Now, consider this. If you owned a JaniKing (a franchise) property maintenance company, you could hire three to four people to work for you, pay them wages, and keep the profits for yourself. In the same eight hours that you would be working a "regular" job, you could make twice the money. And, you can add to your business with more clients and more employees. When you do this, and if you manage your business well, you'll be doubling your income, then tripling it, then quadrupling it, and more (without having to invest much more of your time). Then, if you hit hard times, you can scale back your employees or reduce your prices, but you won't be out of a job.

Now, look once more. Real estate can offer you lifelong profits. What if, instead of maintaining others' properties, you maintained your own? Let's say you scraped together a modest down payment to buy a $100,000 property. You could rent it, maintain it, and collect more money in rent than you pay in your mortgage. Besides the profits tied to the time spent renting and maintaining it, you'll also earn lifelong income not tied to hours worked: appreciation in value. Each year your property earns you another $10,000 to $15,000 in increased value. This money is lifelong income, not dependent on hours spent working.

You say you don't have the capital to buy real estate? No problem. Check out franchises. Some need big bucks, but some don't;

www.franchisesolutions.com helps people choose good ones, but be prepared to devote a full-time effort.

Only want a part-time business? There are businesses you can start for a very reasonable investment. You'll find them in a book entitled, *The Best Home Businesses for the 21st Century: The Inside Information You Need to Know to Select a Home-Based Business That's Right for You,* by Paul Edwards and Sarah Edwards. Their URL is *www. paulandsarah.com.*

Other home-based choices for part-time with lucrative lifelong income are network marketing businesses (a.k.a. multilevel marketing). They can usually be started for a small amount of money. You do need to exercise caution, however, because there are good choices and bad ones in that industry, just as in any other industry. Check out the Direct Selling Association at *www.dsa.org.* If a company is listed there, it meets the first test of credibility.

With a little due diligence, creative thinking, time management, and money, your own business can create a second income stream that will see you through hard times while providing you with a sense of self-satisfaction and fulfillment.

—*Jack Chapman, Lucrative Careers, Inc.*

TIP #95—CONSULTANTS ON THE RISE

One of the single fastest growing professions today is consulting (a.k.a. interim positions, job shopping). As recent as the 1980s, there were only a handful of consultants, most working with one of the large, well-established consulting firms like Andersen, Gemini, and George S. May. Today, the number of consultants has exploded. Why?

Companies have learned that they need subject-matter experts, problem solvers, planners, project managers, advisors, and others. But, they don't need them forever. They want them to come into the company, solve the problem, and then go away. It's that simple. They don't want the lifelong "marriage" that used to exist between company and employee. It is far more attractive to a company to hire you for a specific assignment, pay you well, and then amicably part ways. What's more, if you can keep yourself continually engaged, it can be a great way to make a living. Consulting affords you flexibility in type of project assignments, company affiliations, scheduling, and more, that you simply can't get any other way.

If you are in a position to consider consulting as your next career choice, ask yourself these four critical questions:

1. Can you live with the risk of self-employment? Any new venture takes time and commitment and presents a financial risk. Be sure that you are willing to assume these pressures and responsibilities.

2. Are you really an expert (or pretty close) in the field in which you want to consult? Companies want expert assistance so be sure your credentials are "up to snuff."

3. Can you market your consulting practice? Marketing is just as vital to your success as your professional skills and knowledge. If you can't market your consulting practice, there will be no practice. If marketing is going to be your demise, consider partnering with a marketing professional who can handle all your marketing, sales, and business development activities while you manage the consulting engagements.

4. Are you already overwhelmed in financial commitment and debt? No matter how well planned and managed, any new venture takes time before it makes money. Be sure that you have the financial resources to see yourself through.

If your answers to any of the above four questions make you hesitant to launch your own consulting practice, consider taking a position as a consultant with an established consulting firm. There are now thousands of them, from the major players mentioned earlier to specialty consulting boutiques. Use the Internet as a resource to begin to identify those with which you might like to become affiliated and then begin a full-blown search campaign targeted exclusively to those firms. Through this type of employment, you get the best of both worlds—the excitement and diversity of consulting along with the stability of a weekly paycheck.

—Author's tip

TIP #96—Do You Have What It Takes to Be an Entrepreneur?

If you've ever considered launching your own entrepreneurial venture, now may be just the time. As the once-secure world of corporate employment has disappeared during our lifetimes, the world of entrepreneurship has opened vast new opportunities. However, these opportunities have several stringent requirements:

- You must have money or be able to get some. Starting a business, no matter how closely you watch your dollars, costs money; sometimes, a lot of money. Either you'll need to have your own resources or be able to get the resources elsewhere (e.g., bank loan, private investor, venture capital funding). This can be an extremely difficult and time-consuming effort, even if you've got the best idea since sliced bread.

- You must have money to live on. Not only do you have to fund your new venture, you also have to have the resources to sustain you and your family through the early stages of your new business until the cash begins to flow (assuming that it does).

- You must have a great business concept and a solid business plan. Starting a business isn't a quick decision. It requires intense thought and analysis to determine if your idea can succeed. You must be an economist, financial analyst, accountant, strategic planner, team builder, operations manager, sales producer, and so much more. This book was not intended as a lesson on entrepreneurship. I recommend you review numerous online resources, read books and magazines, talk to other entrepreneurs, and educate yourself about entrepreneurship and all that is required.

- You must be an astute marketer. No matter what your specific business is, you must be able to sell it. Without customers, you have nothing. Therefore, marketing, sales, and business development must be activities that you can either competently manage yourself or for which you are willing to pay for talent.

- You have to learn to live with the risk of self-employment and a risk it is. One week will be great; the next a disaster. Problem after problem will arise, cash flow will be unevenly generated throughout the year, there will be countless unanticipated expenses, your best salesperson will quit without warning, and worse. Ask yourself if you can live on the emotional roller coaster and handle the stress. It's a huge consideration.

And, always remember that the typical entrepreneur is the lady down the street with a small retail store; not Bill Gates. Be realistic about your expectations!

If you're serious about starting your own business, refer to the Entrepreneurial Profile Checklist on the following pages. Take the time to complete this questionnaire to see where you rank on the "entrepreneurial success scale."

—Author's tip

Do You Have the Entrepreneurial Spirit?

Ever considered going into business for yourself? Have some great new product or technology idea? Thinking about starting a consulting practice? Considering starting a business with a friend or colleague? Always contemplating new entrepreneurial ideas and ventures? Striving to be self-employed?

If you answered yes to any of these questions, you'll want to take a few minutes to complete this Entrepreneurial Profile Assessment. It will help you to evaluate whether or not you have the "entrepreneurial spirit and drive" that will be so vital to your success.

To launch a successful venture, you must have the necessary product, service, and/or industry expertise. However, it is just as critical that you be a talented entrepreneur, able to build a company, sell your products and/or services, understand the finances, hire and train the people, solve problems, and make the difficult decisions. You must ask yourself if you're willing to commit to the demands of self-employment—demands on your time, energy, knowledge, and spirit.

Entrepreneurial Profile Assessment

Yes　**No**

☐　☐　Have you clearly defined your expertise and your business concept?

☐　☐　Do you believe in your heart that your proposed business venture will be successful?

☐　☐　Have you identified a specific market for your services and/or products?

☐　☐　Do you know who your competition is, what they do and what they charge?

☐　☐　Have you written a formal business plan?

☐　☐　Have you shared your business concept with others to get their feedback?

☐　☐　Do you have an advertising and marketing plan in place?

☐ ☐ Have you prepared budget, revenue, and income projections?

☐ ☐ Have you sought the advice of an accountant or financial consultant?

☐ ☐ Have you sought legal counsel?

☐ ☐ Are you self-disciplined?

☐ ☐ Do you have grit?

☐ ☐ Do you have an inner drive that propels you?

☐ ☐ Do you have a consistently positive attitude almost 100 percent of the time?

☐ ☐ Are you focused, diligent, and determined?

☐ ☐ Are you charismatic and enthusiastic?

☐ ☐ Do you have a tremendous amount of energy?

☐ ☐ Are you smart?

☐ ☐ Do you have top-flight morals, ethics, and integrity?

☐ ☐ Are you willing to work harder than you ever have before?

☐ ☐ Is your family supportive?

☐ ☐ Can you take constructive criticism without becoming offended?

☐ ☐ Can you think independently?

☐ ☐ Can you make decisions?

☐ ☐ Can you solve problems?

☐ ☐ Do you thrive in challenging and fast-paced environments?

☐ ☐ Can you handle the constant change and realignment that any new venture requires?

☐ ☐ Are you able to work without supervision?

☐ ☐ Can you handle disappointment and then move on?

☐ ☐ Are you willing to learn from your mistakes?

☐ ☐ Do you believe that you can always learn from others?

☐ ☐ Are you well organized?

☐ ☐ Do you have good written communication skills?

☐ ☐ Do you have strong oral communication skills?

☐ ☐ Are you comfortable speaking in public?

☐ ☐ Are you a creative and visionary thinker?

☐ ☐ Are you "hungry" to succeed?

☐ ☐ Are you flexible?

☐ ☐ Do you have the financial resources to support yourself during the start-up phases of your venture?

☐ ☐ Can you persevere through difficult times?

☐ ☐ Can you live comfortably in a high-risk employment situation?

☐ ☐ Do you understand that calculated risks can lead to tremendous rewards?

☐ ☐ Can your mind and your body handle unusually large amounts of stress?

☐ ☐ Does a great deal of your self-image come from your work?

☐ ☐ Do you *really* crave success and self-satisfaction?

☐ ☐ Are you ready *now*?

If you've answered "Yes" to more than 25 of these questions, you have what it takes to be a successful entrepreneur. Take your time, plan well, and move forward steadfastly. Success can be yours if you devote your time, money, drive, knowledge, and spirit.

TIP #97—IT'S OKAY TO RETIRE

If you've put in your 25 or 35 years, traded in your stock options for millions of dollars, or won the lotto, it's okay *not* to work. So much of our lives and our identities are tied directly to what we do in our professional lives that it's often difficult ever to stop working. How many people do you know that have retired, felt underutilized, and returned to work? Quite a few, I would assume. These people never learned to find their real identity—the person within.

We must alter our mindsets and beliefs to appreciate the fact that it really is okay not to have a job. Our lives are so much more than just work. Unfortunately, as the atmosphere of the workplace has become so competitive, it has become difficult not to have a job. People constantly wonder why you're unemployed and what's wrong with you. Rather, they should celebrate the fact that you're past the working stage of your life and now onto much better and more personally fulfilling activities.

To learn how to enjoy the next stage of your life, read the next tip about the third quarter of life. This will help you understand and appreciate all that you can do with your life, knowledge, resources, energy, and ideas.

—Author's tip

TIP #98—HARVESTING THE ABUNDANCE OF THE THIRD QUARTER OF LIFE

The third quarter of life is a period of potential growth and abundance, one that requires a shift away from the productivity focus of the second quarter and long before the fourth quarter takes us into a period of less possibilities and less abundance. You may continue working but your career no longer defines you. Your definition of success changes and you do less charging straight ahead and care more for yourself, others, and the planet. Today, there are no specific age markers for this quarter, because at this point in life much depends on the person and his personal development.

We have received two gifts that our parents and grandparents most likely didn't receive. The first gift is wellness that adds an additional 20 years of life, which should be thought of as being used and harvested *now*. The second gift is relative financial abundance. I know that my basic needs will be met today and tomorrow. I am also finding that my needs are less regarding material things and that my life is becoming less possession oriented.

Here is a graphic of the third quarter and the abundance that can be added to life:

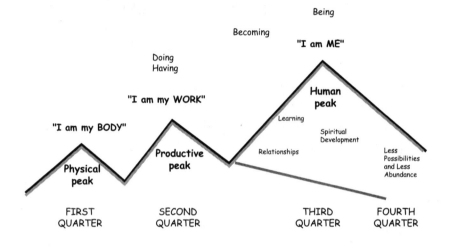

You can see that it can be the most abundant of the four quarters. The theme of the third quarter is "being," which is a more reflective time when we can embrace new friendships, explore our passions, expand our lives, and share our wisdom and our gifts. The activities of the third quarter include engaging the world on your own terms, spiritual development, the deepening of relationships, and active learning. In the third quarter we now have time to enrich and deepen relationships with ourselves, we are more inner focused and we don't have to "keep up with the Jones'." We are more ourselves and less the expectations of others. It is also a time of enriching relationships with other persons in our lives, including spouses/partners, children and grandchildren, and in the world of today and tomorrow, our parents. This quarter is a time for collecting and sharing our life stories, personal history, and wisdom.

In the third quarter, learning can occur in many ways other than sitting in a classroom. The continuation and possible acceleration of learning is a great stimulant in the third quarter. It is truly lifetime learning coupled with travel, Elderhostels, the Internet, tutors, tapes, and so forth. We take charge of our self-directed learning and find others we can learn with and from.

Spiritual development may include pursuing questions of faith, the meaning of life, and celebration. There may be times of doubt and leaps of faith. There can also be legacy questions of what we have done to create a better world and what we leave behind. These may involve not property, but rather our personal history, wisdom, dreams, and leadership contributions.

If the third quarter is so potentially abundant, why do so many skip it and go on to the fourth quarter? They are using old life maps which say that you are just supposed to "stay busy." A life map for today, based on your uniqueness, can help lead you into the third quarter and guide you to success. Much in our life maps is inherited from our parents and relatives and may not serve as the best guide for today's and tomorrow's worlds. There are no more mile markers that work; the markers about how we are to live at different periods in our lives are gone. There are no age markers, lifetime employers, or places of no change. We are in the wake of the whitewater of life and the old rules don't work anymore. We have to learn to create our own new life maps as we and the world change.

How do you create a life map? First, start with listing your polished skills as well as your nascent (but little-used) skills. Add your competencies and achievements, including those from a young age and years past. Ask 10 other persons you know to give you a list of the qualities that are unique about you. List your wisdom that may be helpful to others and be generous with yourself in creating your list. Then tap into your hopes and dreams to identify the message within you that you must tell the world before the end of your life. List your passions and your concerns. Add your competencies, including those from a young age and years past. Ask yourself "What would it be like if _____?" or "With my magic wand, what would I heal or improve in the world?" It's a time to be visionary.

Career, in terms of discovering and using your gifts to be engaged with the world, is for a lifetime. This doesn't necessarily mean that you have to work for the rest of your life, but it means to be engaged with the world on your terms and giving your gifts. Enter the third quarter of life, explore all the possibilities for more abundance, and open undiscovered new doors in your life.

If this sounds like a big step to take, look around for other people who might serve as models for your new life map, but remember that your life map should be designed specifically for you, based on the assessment information that you have developed for yourself. If you want some help, there are life/personal coaches who can guide you. A good selection tip is to ask if the coach has third quarter of life experience and if they have a larger view of the world than you presently have.

—Richard L. Haid, Ph.D., PCC, Richard Haid & Associates

TIP #99—New Careers on the Horizon

Just five years ago, no one had ever heard of a website designer, a JAVA scripter or a chief knowledge officer. There were no intellectual capital analysts, no HTML programmers, and no new media specialists. Ten years ago, there were no organizational development consultants or employee assistance professionals. As corporations, corporate cultures, and the entire employment market have undergone dramatic changes, redefined themselves, and gone through a massive period of technological growth, new positions have emerged to meet new demands.

To ensure that you and your career are always on the leading edge, you must know what is going on. What are the newest developments in the workplace, what new industries are hot, what new positions are evolving, and what do you anticipate will happen in the future? Since none of us have a crystal ball, we have to rely on intelligence we receive from others—in newspapers and magazines, online, through conversation, and through our own diligent research. To stay on top, you must know where on top will be—this year, next year, and five years from now.

If you follow future trends, you most likely know that the following are the key industries for anticipated growth over the next 10 to 20 years. Be sure to understand that these are trend projections and *not* factual information.

- Biomedical technology and engineering
- Scientific research and development
- Information, telecommunications, and media technologies
- Educational services and products
- Oceanographic exploration and development
- Alternative transportation

If these, or related professions, are of interest to you, consider taking a few classes to begin shifting your career in the direction of anticipated changes. But, remember that flexibility is key and that no industry today is ever recession-proof. You've personally seen the evidence of that.

—Author's tip

Tip #100—Control Your Destiny

The old lifetime contract for employment is long gone. Job security is a thing of the past—at least in terms of a guarantee or even expectation of employment. But, in many ways, the new world of employment is more exciting, more personally rewarding, and offers more scope for your creative energies.

You no longer have to be a victim to a corporate strategy or vision that you don't agree with. If your company suffers from poor leadership, mediocre product quality, lack of innovation, or serious competitive deficiencies, you can take your talents to another organization.

This new world does require some mental shifts on your part. First, and most importantly, you must acknowledge and accept the fact that your career is in your own hands. Then you need to understand your value in the marketplace and, throughout your career, gather evidence of your ability to help companies be more successful, more profitable, and more competitive. This evidence—which you can translate into accomplishment statements on your resume and success stories during your interviews—is what will make you attractive to new employers.

It is empowering to know that you control your destiny. When you take control, chart your course, and proactively manage your career, you will find self-worth, self-satisfaction, and self-esteem.

—*Louise Kursmark, CPRW, JCTC, CEIP, CCM,*
Best Impression Career Services, Inc.

TIP #101—ALWAYS REMEMBER WHO YOU WORK FOR

Etch these words into your mind. You work for yourself and your family, *not* for who writes your paycheck.

If you remember this concept, it will keep you focused on what's most important about your career . . . that you build, steer, and proactively manage it in the direction in which you'll find both personal and professional fulfillment. Don't be a victim of your career by letting it happen to you. Rather, take control and lead yourself to success.

Use the "I Am Prepared" checklist on the following page as a reminder of what is critical to moving your career forward—today and in years to come.

—*Author's tip*

"I am Prepared" Checklist

Review this list on a regular basis to:

- Keep yourself motivated.
- Keep you and your career on-track.
- Remind yourself that these are the *really* important things that will move your career forward.
- Remind yourself of your commitment to proactive, lifelong career management.

□ I understand that I must **MARKET** my career to move it forward.

□ I strive constantly to maintain a **PROFESSIONAL** image and style.

□ I am committed to my own **PROFESSIONAL GROWTH AND DEVELOPMENT** to further my skills and my professional options.

□ I understand that my career will always be in **TRANSITION**.

□ I am committed to **INTROSPECTION** and always being aware of what motivates and influences me to my peak performance.

□ I am **INDEPENDENT** and **SELF-RELIANT**.

□ I am always **PREPARED** with current job search materials in the event that I should unexpectedly need them.

□ I am **MOTIVATED, ENTHUSIASTIC**, and **POSITIVE**.

□ I can quickly, confidently, and accurately communicate my **VALUE** to a prospective employer.

□ I understand the importance of my **RELATIONSHIPS**—with colleagues, coworkers, supervisors, managers, executives, and all others in my careers community.

□ I appreciate the fact that the **PERCEPTION** others have of me is a key contributor to my success.

□ I am 100 percent **HONEST** in all of my professional and career endeavors.

- [ ] I know that **NETWORKING** is vital to my lifelong career success and progression.

- [ ] I realize that I must be **TECHNOLOGICALLY SAVVY** to compete in today's job-search market.

- [ ] I am **ORGANIZED, THOROUGH**, and **EFFICIENT**.

- [ ] I am able to maintain an appropriate **PERSPECTIVE** on my career and how it complements my entire life.

- [ ] I am **INNOVATIVE** and **VERSATILE**.

- [ ] I understand the **COMPETITIVE** nature of the employment market and I am ready to WIN!

- [ ] I have impeccable **ETHICS** and **INTEGRITY**.

- [ ] I understand that my career satisfaction is based on more than **MONEY**.

- [ ] I am the only one that truly has **POWER** and **CONTROL** over my life and my career.

- [ ] I am **DETERMINED** and committed to my own **CAREER SUCCESS**.

Contributors

For full contact information (address, telephone, email, and website) for each contributor, visit *www.cminstitute.com*, click on Membership Directory, and type in the last name of the individual. In many instances you will also find a professional biography for that contributor.

Vivian Belen, NCRW, CPRW, JCTC, The Job Search Specialist

Kathy Black, MBA, JCTC, Career Recipes

Arnold Boldt, CPRW, JCTC, Arnold-Smith Associates

Diana Bradford, CPRW, JCTC, CareerBound

Ann Brody, MSW, Career Solutions, Inc.

Bob Bronstein, MBA, Pro/File Research

Jack Chapman, Lucrative Careers, Inc.

Pierre Daunic, PhD, CCM, R.L. Stevens & Associates, Inc.

Candace Davies, BBA, CPRW, Cando Career Coaching & Resume Writing

Kirsten Dixson, JCTC, CPRW, CEIP, New Leaf Career Solutions

Debbie Ellis, CPRW, Phoenix Career Group

Joyce Fortier, MBA, CCM, CPRW, JCTC, Create Your Career

Arthur Frank, MBA, Resumes "R" Us

Louise Garver, MA, CMP, JCTC, CPRW, Career Directions

Norm Gavlick, Gavlick Personnel Services, Inc.

Susan Guarneri, NCCC, NCC, LPC, JCTC, CPRW, CEIP, CCM, Guarneri Associates/Resumagic

Darrell Gurney, CPC, JCTC, A Permanent Success National Career Coaching & Search Partners

Michele Haffner, CPRW, JCTC, Advanced Resume Services

Richard Haid, PhD, PCC, Adult Mentor, Richard Haid & Associates

E. René Hart, CPRW, Executive Career Solutions

Beverly Harvey, CPRW, JCTC, CCM, Beverly Harvey Resume & Career Services

Lynn Hughes, MA, CPRW, CEIP, A Resume and Career Service, Inc.

Nancy Karvonen, CPRW, CCM, JCTC, CEIP, A Better Word & Resume

Fran Kelley, MA, CPRW, SPHR, JCTC, The Resume Works

Shanna Kemp, MEd, IJCTC, CPRW, CCM, Kemp Career Services

Elie Klachkin, MS, JCTC, Impex Services, Inc.

Cynthia Kraft, CPRW, JCTC, CCM, Executive Essentials

Anne Kramer, CPRW, Alpha Bits

Louise Kursmark, CPRW, JCTC, CEIP, CCM, Best Impression Career Services, Inc.

Rolande LaPointe, CPC, CIPC, CPRW, IJCTC, CCM, RO-LAN Associates, Inc.

Linsey Levine, MS Career Development, JCTC, CareerCounsel

Susan Luff Chritton, MEd, NCCC, CRPCC, Pathways/Right Management Consultants

Denise Lupardo, Denise's Office Support & Resumes

Ross Macpherson, MA, CPRW, CEIP, JCTC, Career Quest

Linda Matias, JCTC, CEIP, CareerStrides

Kathleen McInerney, CEIP, JCTC, Career Edge, Inc.

Jan Melnik, CPRW, CCM, Absolute Advantage

Nicole Miller, BA, RRP, CPRW, IJCTC, Mil-Roy Consultants

Meg Montford, CCM, CPRW, Abilities Enhanced

William Murdock, CPRW, The Employment Coach

Debra O'Reilly, CPRW, JCTC, CEIP, ResumeWriter.com

Don Orlando, MBA, CPRW, JCTC, CCM, The McLean Group

Barb Poole, CPRW, Hire Imaging

Don Skipper, MS, MMAS, CCM, R.L. Stevens & Associates, Inc.

Laurie Smith, CPRW, IJCTC, Creative Keystrokes Executive Resume Service

Deborah Wile Dib, CCM, NCRW, CPRW, CEIP, JCTC, Advantage Resumes of New York

Janice Worthington, CPRW, JCTC, CEIP, Worthington Career Services

Karen Wrigley, CPRW, JCTC, AMW Career & Resume Services

About the Author

Wendy S. Enelow is the founder and president of the Career Masters Institute, a training and development association for career professionals worldwide. Previously, as the founder/director of The Advantage, Inc., Wendy built one of the nation's largest and most successful firms offering resume writing, career coaching, and job search services to top executives worldwide. To date she has authored 12 career publications and is best known for her "$100,000+" series of job-search books. Wendy speaks and trains nationwide on resume writing, career marketing, career management, and entrepreneurship. Born in Pittsburgh, PA, she spent her high school years in West Africa and Italy, is a summa cum laude graduate of the University of Maryland, and has been a successful entrepreneur for more than 25 years.